B-17 Flying Fortress

Written by David Doyle

In Action®

Squadron Signal® Publications

Cover Art by Don Greer

Line Illustrations by Matheu Spraggins

(Front Cover) Certainly the most celebrated B-17, the *Memphis Belle,* B-17F-10-BO 41-24485, fought through 25 grueling missions over Europe. Hollywood director William Wyler documented one of the plane's last missions in a color film that, together with the crew's subsequent cross-country war bond tour, made *Memphis Belle* a household name. Today, the fabled aircraft resides at the National Museum of the United States Air Force near Dayton, Ohio.

(Back Cover) *Milk Wagon* a B-17G-7-BO with the 447th Bomb Group was a veteran of 129 missions without ever having to abort due to a mechanical issue – a tribute to her ground crew. The aircraft was delivered 18 May 1944 and was on station 20 June 1944. She was sold from scrap at Kingman, Arizona, on 21 November 1945.

About the In Action® Series

In Action® books, despite the title of the genre, are books that trace the development of a single type of aircraft, armored vehicle, or ship from prototype to the final production variant. Experimental or "one-off" variants can also be included. Our first *In Action®* book was printed in 1971.

Hard Cover ISBN 978-0-89747-632-4
Soft Cover ISBN 978-0-89747-622-5

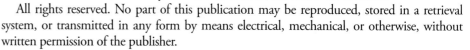

Proudly Printed in the U.S.A.
Copyright 2010, 2011 Squadron/Signal Publications
1115 Crowley Drive, Carrollton, TX 75006-1312 U.S.A.

Military/Combat Photographs and Snapshots

If you have any photos of aircraft, armor, soldiers, or ships of any nation, particularly wartime snapshots, why not share them with us and help make Squadron/Signal's books all the more interesting and complete in the future? Any photograph sent to us will be copied and returned. Electronic images are preferred. The donor will be fully credited for any photos used. Please send them to:

Squadron/Signal Publications
1115 Crowley Drive
Carrollton, TX 75006-1312 U.S.A.
www.SquadronSignalPublications.com

(Title Page) The B-17 was the mainstay of the U.S. strategic bombing campaign in Europe during WWII. Designed in 1935, the B-17 was a significant advance in multi-engine heavy bomber aircraft. Here, a formation of B-17Gs of the 381st Bomb Group, 532nd Bomb Squadron, is escorted by a P-51B (background). In the foreground is *Patches,* B-17G-70-BO serial number 43-37675, which was later downed over Berlin on 28 March 1945. The red areas on the wings and stabilizers mark these Flying Fortresses as part of the 1st Combat Bomb Wing. *Patches* was fitted with a Cheyenne tail turret. (National Archives)

Acknowledgments

This book would have been impossible without the generous help many friends – old and new – specifically: Tom Kailbourn; Stan Piet; Brett Stolle and the staff of the National Museum of the United States Air Force; Larry Davis; Charles Bordner; the staff of the National Archives; the Dyersburg Army Air Base Memorial Association (DAABMA); and the team at the Air Force Historical Research Agency. Special thanks go to my wife Denise, who spent many hours alongside me in musty archives, gathering this material.

Introduction

The B-17 Flying Fortress is arguably the iconic bomber of WWII. Designated Model 299 by its designer, Boeing aircraft, a total of 12,731 of the heavy bombers were produced over a 10-year period. Not only Boeing, but also Douglas Aircraft and the Vega subsidiary of Lockheed turned out B-17s. Although some B-17s remained in Air Force inventory into the 1950s, these planes were just a few air rescue, transport, and target drone aircraft. Its legendary role as a bomber wrapped up on VJ Day. Nevertheless, the B-17 was central to the development of the entire strategic bombing concept that would dominate the American bomber concept for no less than five decades. With such a storied history, and having played such a key role in America's war effort, it is not surprising that the Flying Fortress and the men that crewed, serviced, and built it have been the subjects of hundreds of books. Having seen the B-17 in *12 O'Clock High,* my interest was piqued when my father took me to a showing of the then-recently rediscovered 1943 film *Memphis Belle* by William Wyler. Most shocking to me – the film was in color. Thus began my search for photographs and information about the B-17 – particularly color photos.

The purpose of this book is, through 200+ photos and drawings, to present a visual overview of the development and use of the B-17 from the first flight of the model 299 in July 1935 to the career of the B-17H, the last of the wartime Fortresses.

The B-17, or Model 299, was created in response to Army Air Corps Circular 35-26. This document had called for a fly-off competition amongst designs of multi-engine bombers having a top speed of 200 to 250 miles per hour at 10,000 feet, a cruising speed of 170 to 220 miles per hour at 10,000 feet, a service ceiling of 20,000 to 25,000 feet and an endurance of six to ten hours at cruise level.

The Model 299 was the sole four-engine competitor, flying against the Martin Model 146 (a modified B-10B) and the Douglas B-18A. The performance of the 299 excelled, and it appeared sure to win when tragedy struck. Among the advancements in the 299 design were control surface locks used while the aircraft was on the ground. Wright Field chief test pilot, Major Ployer Peter Hill, flying the aircraft for the first time, failed to completely release the control locks, resulting in the crash of the 299 and the deaths of Hill and Boeing chief test pilot Leslie Tower, who was an observer on the flight. In addition to their lives, the tragedy cost Boeing the lucrative production contract. The Army Air Corps had liked the plane, however. On 30 October 1935, the very day of the crash, Brigadier General Augustine Warner Robins, chief of the Air Material Command, called the War Department to recommend that, despite the crash, 13 of the big Boeings be bought under the experimental provisions of Section K of the National Defense Act (1926). Unknown to Robins, at the same time General Frank M. Andrews, commander of General Headquarters Air Force, sent a cable to the same effect. Per their (and other) advice, 13 test models of Boeing's new Flying Fortress received funding. The lessons taught by these aircraft would prove crucial for the air war soon to unfold in Europe.

Note: For consistency in USAAF unit designations, group precedes squadron (e.g., 5th Bomb Group, 72nd Bomb Squadron) - "Bomb" has been used in unit designations in lieu of "Bombardment."

The Wright Field trials of 1935 were won by the twin-engine Douglas DB-1, which flew against the four-engine Boeing Model 299. When the production order for the DB-1 was placed, it was designated the B-18 (Boeing's Model 299 was given the B-17 designation when an order for 12 trial airplanes was placed). The B-18 was given the nod as a result of the crash through pilot error, of the Model 299, and also due to price ($58,500 vs. $99,620 for the Model 299). Remarkably, an improved model of the B-18, the B-18A remained in production through 1939. Essentially a redesigned DC-2 airliner, the B-18 was, as a practical matter, obsolete when it left the assembly line. (National Museum of the United States Air Force)

1935 Bomber Competition

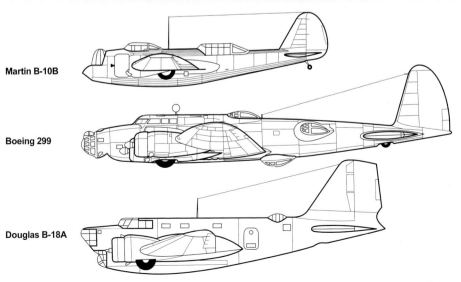

Martin B-10B

Boeing 299

Douglas B-18A

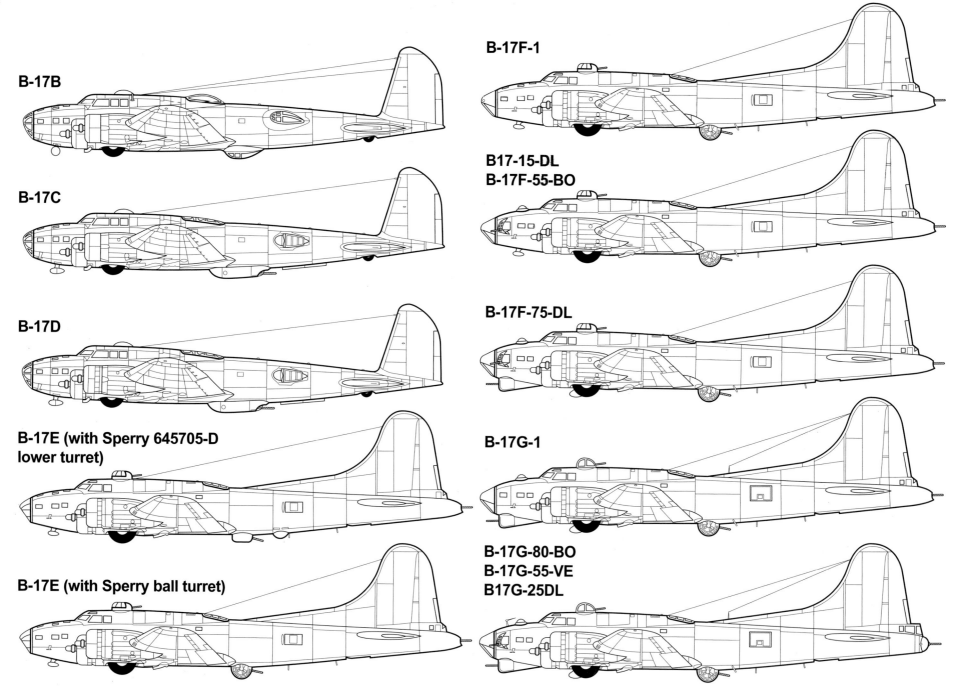

B-17B

B-17C

B-17D

B-17E (with Sperry 645705-D
lower turret)

B-17E (with Sperry ball turret)

B-17F-1

B17-15-DL
B-17F-55-BO

B-17F-75-DL

B-17G-1

B-17G-80-BO
B-17G-55-VE
B17G-25DL

Model 299

The Model 299 was the prototype of the B-17 and Boeing's entry in a competition for a new bomber announced by the U.S. Army Air Corps in May 1934. Design work started in June 1934 and the aircraft was completed on 18 July 1935. It featured four 750-horsepower Pratt & Whitney R-1690 radial engines, a clear nose with a machine gun turret on top, and a raised cockpit enclosure that would carry over to the B-17. (National Museum of the United States Air Force)

Unlike the B-17, where the bombardier's window was toward the bottom of the clear nose, the bombardier's window in the Model 299 was at the rear of an indentation in the underside of the fuselage to the rear of the clear nose. The main landing gear was somewhat complex, incorporating dual struts mounted to the rear of the landing gear well and a double yoke and actuator forming a drag brace to the front of the struts. (National Museum of the United States Air Force)

Following its completion, the Model 299 was flown from the Boeing plant in Seattle to Wright Field, Ohio, for testing. During testing on 30 October 1935, the Model 299 was destroyed in a crash, costing the lives of the pilot and copilot. The cause: pilot failure to unlock the elevators before takeoff. However, the aircraft had performed well enough during the tests to earn Boeing a contract to produce 13 service test bombers to be designated the Y1B-17. (National Museum of the United States Air Force)

A crowd views the completed Model 299 in front of a Boeing hangar in Seattle. In addition to the clear turret on the nose, this aircraft had blisters for machine guns in the ventral and dorsal positions and on each side of the waist. The engine nacelles lacked cowl flaps, a feature that would not be introduced until the B-17D. There is an oval entry door to the rear of the right wing and a ladder is set up below the door. The tail number, X13372, is a civil registration number. No army serial number was assigned to this aircraft, since it never became government property, remaining instead Boeing property. For the same reason, it was never officially classified as the XB-17, but retained the designation Model 299.

Experimental Specifications by Make

	Boeing Model 299	Martin Model 146	Douglas DB-1
Armament	Five .30-cal. or five .50-cal. machine guns	Three .30-cal. guns	Three .30-cal. guns (in nose, ventral and dorsal positions)
Bomb load	4,800 lbs.	2,260 lbs.	4,400 lbs.
Engine	Four Pratt & Whitney R-1690 radials of 750 h.p. each	Two Wright R-1820-33s of 775 h.p. each	Two Wright R-1820-53s of 1,000 h.p. each
Crew	Eight	Four	Six
Top speed	236 m.p.h.	234 m.p.h. at 13,500 ft.	215 m.p.h. at 15,000 ft.
Cruising speed	140 m.p.h.	183 m.p.h.	167 m.p.h.
Range	3,010 miles	1,370 miles	2,100 miles
Service ceiling	24,620 ft.	24,200 ft.	23,900 ft.
Wing Span	103 ft. 9 3/8 in.	70 ft. 6 in.	89 ft. 6 in.
Length	68 ft. 9 in.	44 ft. 9 in.	57 ft. 10 in.
Height	14 ft. 11 15/16 in.	15 ft. 5 in.	15 ft. 2 in.
Weight	32,432 lbs. loaded	14,700 lbs. loaded	27,000 lbs. loaded

Following the promising performance of the Model 299, the Army Air Corps ordered 13 further bombers from Boeing in January 1936. Initially designated the YB-17, this model was subsequently redesignated the Y1B-17. It resembled the Model 299 but was equipped with Wright R-1820-39 Cyclone engines and single-strut main landing gear, and had other modifications, including as an improved oxygen system. (National Museum of the United States Air Force)

A Y1B-17 in Olive Drab and Neutral Gray camouflage revs up its engines. Capable of achieving 950 horsepower each, the four Wright R-1820-39 Cyclone radial engines provided almost 25 percent more power than the Pratt & Whitney R-1690 engines of the Model 299. Below the single cheek window is a pitot tube. Above and to the rear of the cockpit are a radio antenna mast and a circular radio direction finder (RDF) antenna. (Library of Congress)

Whereas the Model 299 had protruding, tube-shaped landing lights on the leading edges of the wings, the Y1B-17 had recessed landing lights with a flush clear cover that was rectangular in shape when viewed from the front. The flaps were changed from the metal ones of the Model 299 to fabric-covered. Also, the Y1B-17 had a redesigned, tubular-shaped air intake/engine exhaust shroud on top of each of the engine nacelles. (National Museum of the United States Air Force)

B-17 Specifications by Model

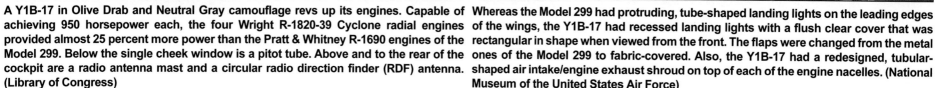

	Y1B-17	Y1B-17A	B-17B	B-17C	B-17D	B-17E	B-17F	B-17G
Armament	5 x .30-cal.	5 x .30-cal.	1 x .30 + 6 x .50 cal.	1 x .30 + 6 x .50 cal.	1 x .30 + 6 x .50 cal.	8 x .50 cal.	11 x .50 cal.	12 x .50 cal.
Bomb Load	4,800 lbs.	4,800 lbs.	4,400 lbs.	4,800 lbs.	4,800 lbs.	4,200 lbs.	8,000 lbs	8,000 lbs
Engines (4 x)	Wright R-1820-39 930 h.p.	Wright R-1820-51 1000 h.p.	Wright R-1820-51 1,200 h.p.	Wright R-1820-65 1,200 h.p.	Wright R-1820-65 1,200 h.p.	Wright R-1820-65 1,200 h.p.	Wright R-1820-97 1,200 hp	Wright R-1820-97 1,200 hp
Max speed	256 mph @ 14,000 ft	295 mph @ 25,000 ft	292 mph @ 25,000 ft	323 mph @ 25,000 ft	323 mph @ 25,000 ft	317 mph @ 25,000 ft	325 mph @ 25,000 ft	302 mph @ 25,000 ft
Cruise speed	175 mph	183 mph	225 mph	227 mph	227 mph	226 mph	160 mph	160 mph
Service Ceiling	30,600 feet	38,000 feet	36,000 feet	37,000 ft	37,000 ft	36,000 ft	37,500 feet	35,600 feet
Range	3,320 miles	3,600 miles	3,600 miles	3,400 miles	3,400 miles	3,200 miles	4.220 miles	3,400 miles
Wing Span	103' 9"	103' 9"	103' 9"	103' 9"	103' 9"	103' 9"	103' 9"	103' 9"
Length	68' 9"	68' 9"	67' 10"	67' 11"	67' 11"	73' 10"	74' 9"	74' 9"
Height	15' 0"	15' 0"	15' 0"	15' 5"	15' 5"	19' 2"	19' 1"	19' 1"
Weight	34,873 lbs. gross	37,000 lbs. gross	38,000 lbs.	48,500 lbs. gross	48,500 lbs. gross	51,000 lbs. gross	56.500 lbs.	65,500 lbs.
Number built/converted	13	1	39	38	42	512	3,405	8,680

The clear nose of the Y1B-17 was on a race mount, so the entire structure could be rotated to position the machine gun turret on the bottom for firing at enemy aircraft to the lower front. The Y1B-17 also mounted an unusually tall antenna mast to the rear of the cockpit. (National Museum of the United States Air Force)

A view of the right side of the same aircraft shows how subtle and streamlined the ventral turret and the waist turrets were. On the side of the fuselage above the ventral turret was a side door in which was a small, rectangular window. This aircraft bore the markings "U.S. Army" under the wings and the national star roundel under the right wing. The horizontal tail stripes were red and white, while the vertical stripe was blue. (National Museum of the United States Air Force)

The Y1B-17 retained the bomber's window in a recess under the fuselage, and from the front, this arrangement gave the bomber a sharkmouth appearance. Rather than the trapezoidal window of the Model 299, it was now triangular. Spinners have been attached to the propellers of this aircraft. Almost lost in the shadows under the fuselage is the ventral turret, a teardrop-shaped blister similar to the waist and dorsal turrets. (National Museum of the United States Air Force)

The single oleo strut of the Y1B-17's left main landing gear is visible. To the front of the strut are a V-shaped drag brace and a small landing-gear door. The aircraft has Hamilton Standard fixed-pitch propellers. There are no dome shells containing the pitch-adjusting mechanisms on the propeller hubs. (National Museum of the United States Air Force)

Twelve Y1B-17s were assigned to the 2nd Bomb Group, and three of those bombers, of the 49th Bomb Squadron, under command of Lieutenant Colonel Robert Olds, undertook a successful training mission to locate the Italian luxury liner Rex 800 miles off the coast of New York City on 12 May 1938. Navigator for this mission, which proved that the Air Corps was a viable offensive force with a long and powerful reach, was First Lieutenant Curtis LeMay. (National Museum of the United States Air Force)

The USAAC caption of this photograph identifies the aircraft as the Y1B-17A in flight near Mount Rainier, Washington, on 28 February 1938, but the Y1B-17A did not make its maiden flight until 28 April 1938. Given the differences in appearance between this aircraft and the documented photos of the Y1B-17A, it is possible that this aircraft is a Y1B-17. There is a Wright Field insignia aft of the waist blister. (National Museum of the United States Air Force)

Originally assigned to the 20th Bomb Squadron, 2nd Bomb Group, this Y1B-17 was photographed in a prominent, five-color camouflage scheme during GHQ Air Force Antiaircraft maneuvers in May 1938. The water-based paint, consisting of Light Blue, Sea Green, Dark Olive Drab, Dark Green, and Neutral Gray, already shows signs of wearing off down to the aluminum skin. (National Museum of the United States Air Force)

In an original color view of an early Flying Fortress, a low sun silhouettes a Y1B-17 on Langley Field, Virginia. The antenna mast and the RDF loop antenna protrude above the fuselage to the rear of the cockpit. The Y1, rather than the simple Y, designation of these aircraft is indicative of a funding source outside of normal fiscal year procurement. (Library of Congress)

The airframe that became the Y1B-17A was originally ordered as a static test Y1B-17. But on 6 July 1937 while under command of Lieutenant William Bentley, the fully test-instrument equipped ninth Y1B-17 (sn 36-157) suddenly and unexpectedly went through a violent series of maneuvers while flying on autopilot. Lieutenant Bentley was able to regain control of the aircraft, resume normal flight and land safely. Subsequent analysis of airframe and data recorders indicated that the ordeal had resulted in a partial failure of the upper-inter spar. Icing conditions had caused the autopilot inadvertently to put the aircraft into a spin, producing G-forces of 3.67 G – or two-thirds of the aircraft's safety margin.

This unintended severe flight-testing on the 36-157 meant that the static testing planned for the 14th airframe, a static test article, was not needed. The airframe then became a test bed for a variety of turbosupercharged engine configurations. In the initial installation, the turbines were mounted atop the nacelles, but in subsequent tests moved to their now-familiar location on the underside of the nacelles. This location presented challenges on the inboard engines due to the presence of the main landing gear. To overcome these difficulties, the manifolds of engines 2 and 3 exited the nacelles at 4 and 8 o'clock respectively, and then reentered the nacelle behind the main landing housing. Turbosuperchargers would feature on all subsequent Flying Fortresses.

The turbo-superchargers significantly increased the maximum speed and service ceiling of the Y1B-17A. Boeing took the initiative of self-funding the supercharger experiments, but their boldness yielded great benefits, as turbo-supercharged engines became the norm in American heavy bombers in World War II. Although the superchargers are not readily seen in this photo, exhaust stains from them are visible below the nacelles. (National Museum of the United States Air Force)

The Y1B-17A was essentially an additional Y1B-17 aircraft converted to a test bed for a turbo-supercharger installation. The aircraft, equipped with Wright R-1820-51 engines was photographed during tests at Wright Field in early 1939. By this time, the superchargers had been moved from the top of the engine nacelles, where they caused severe buffeting, to below the nacelles, where their performance was smoother. (National Museum of the United States Air Force)

The final location of the turbo-superchargers in the Y1B-17A below the engine nacelles coincided with the location of the superchargers in production B-17s. From the outboard engines, the exhaust lines were routed inside the nacelles to the superchargers, but on the inboard engines, the exhaust lines were diverted outside, to skirt around the landing gear wells, before reentering the nacelles and completing their routes to the superchargers. (National Museum of the United States Air Force)

The aircraft commander's blister on B-17B serial number 38-211 was offset to the right of the centerline aft of the cockpit, a characteristic of the -B model. The plane number, MD 105, was repeated on the upper left wing. With the dorsal blister turret deleted, the deck aft of the cockpit began to resemble the final appearance of the Flying Fortress. A "football" type RDF antenna was installed below the nose, replacing the loop antenna. (Stan Piet collection)

The Army Air Corps ordered 10 B-17Bs in November 1937, and shortly thereafter exercised an option for 29 more. The first B-17B took flight on 27 June 1939, having been significantly delayed by teething problems with the GE turbosuperchargers. Boeing delivered the complete order of 39 aircraft to the Army Air Corps between 29 July 1939 and 30 March 1940. In a continuous effort to refine the bomber, many changes were introduced to the new B-17B. One immediately noticeable difference on the new model was its restyled nose. The "greenhouse turret" and belly bomb-aiming window were replaced with a built-up nose with flat bomb-aiming panel. The new nose shortened the overall length of the aircraft by about seven inches and would remain in use through the B-17E models.

Beneath the wings of the B-17B were enlarged flaps, which were now made of metal. The surface area of the ailerons was reduced at this time, and on the leading edges of the wings could be found intake slots for the supercharger induction. On the upper surfaces of the wing, aft of the main spar, eight slots were added for intercooler air exhaust.

The cowling was redesigned, based on experiments with the Y1B-17A. The engine exhausts were routed along the left side of the engines mounted on the left wing, and the right side of the engines mounted on the right wing. Hydraulic brakes appeared on the B-17B, replacing the pneumatic brakes used previously. The rudder was enlarged, improving control of the aircraft. Unlike its predecessors, the B-17B's propellers were not fitted with spinners, a feature that would only appear again on the XB-38.

The cost of the B-17B would be a contentious subject, with the Air Corps wanting to pay $198,000 per aircraft, rather than the previously agreed $205,000. Only after Boeing threatened to withdraw from strategic bomber production did the Air Corps relent. Even at that, Boeing later determined that it lost $12,000 per B-17B delivered.

The army issued Boeing an initial contract for 10 B-17Bs on 3 August 1937. The B-17B was similar in layout to the Y1B-17, but with turbo-superchargers, a new clear nose, elimination of the notch for the bombardier's window under the nose, and an aircraft commander's observation blister aft of the cockpit. The B-17C waist window has been retrofitted to the second aircraft seen here in line at March Field, California, in May 1940. (National Museum of the United States Air Force)

YB-17 to B-17B Developments

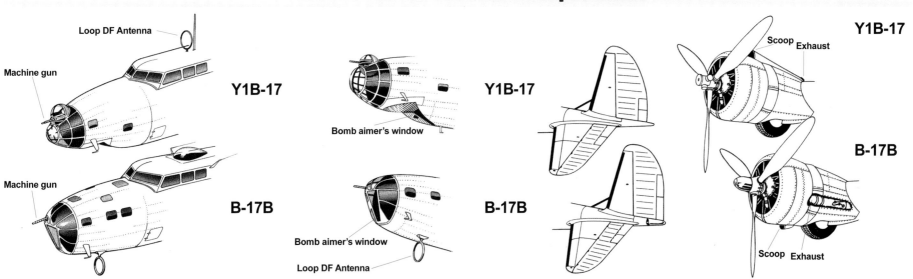

Loop DF Antenna

Machine gun

Y1B-17

Machine gun

B-17B

Bomb aimer's window

Y1B-17

Bomb aimer's window

Loop DF Antenna

B-17B

Y1B-17

B-17B

Y1B-17

Scoop Exhaust

B-17B

Scoop Exhaust

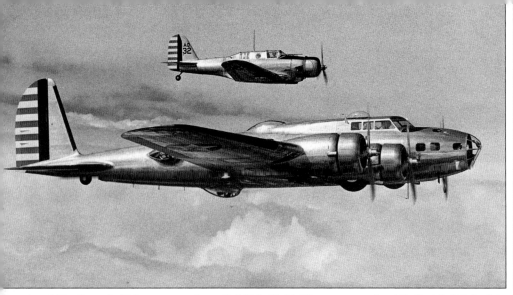

A Northrop A-17A accompanies a B-17B in flight. The army received its first B-17B in July 1939, and a total of 39 of these aircraft were delivered, serving with two bombardment groups. The radio antenna mast aft of the cockpit was eliminated to make room for the observation blister. In addition, the navigator now shared space with the bombardier in the nose, and there was a new arrangement of cheek windows in the nose. (DAABMA)

Photographed on 27 July 1939, the B-17B retained the same waist and ventral blister turrets as employed on the Y1B-17 but substituted a newly designed dorsal turret. The B-17B was the first Flying Fortress to be equipped with the top-secret and highly accurate Norden bomb sight. A radio antenna mast protruded from the fuselage immediately to the rear of the aft cockpit window, and the RDF antenna was relocated to under the nose. (National Museum of the United States Air Force)

The B-17B is the first operational Flying Fortress to serve with the U.S. Army Air Corps. Its flaps have been changed back to aluminum-skinned, the vertical tail is increased in size, and the clear turret on the nose has been eliminated in favor of a socket mount for a machine gun in the clear nose. Propellers are variable-pitch. This particular B-17B is equipped with Wright R-1820-50 engines, although other B-17Bs received R-1820-51s. (National Museum of the United States Air Force)

This B-17B, serial number 38-211, was the first of that model to fly. Subsequently, the Material Division at Wright Airfield replaced the blister turrets, retrofitting this bomber with revised clear panels to test new mounts for defensive weapons that would become standard on the B-17C. The black arrow with yellow border was the symbol of Wright Airfield. "MD" under the tail number stood for Material Division. (Stan Piet collection)

A small, black antiglare panel was painted to the front of the windshield on B-17B number 38-211, and black deicing boots are present on the leading edges of the wings. This aircraft later was lost in a crash after stalling in a climb several miles from its home base of Hendricks Field, Sebring, Florida, on 22 October 1942. It is thought that the student pilot flying the plane was attempting the climb to avoid another B-17. (Stan Piet collection)

The B-17C was similar to the B-17B, with a few modifications. The dorsal blister turret gave way to a more streamlined, sliding clear panel, the ventral blister turret was replaced with a "bathtub" type gun mount, and each of these positions mounted either a .30- or .50-caliber machine gun. The waist machine gun blisters were replaced by flush-mounted, teardrop-shaped panels, and the engines were upgraded to Wright 1820-65s. (Air Force Historical Research Agency)

When the British and French purchasing commissions inspected a Flying Fortress at Boeing in 1940, based on their experiences combating the Luftwaffe, they found the B-17's defense armament and positions inadequate. In response to this input, the B-17C featured new waist gun installations – the "blisters" giving way to streamlined hatches that afforded the gunners more visibility and maneuverability. At the same time the belly blister weapons installation was replaced with a larger "bathtub" that housed a .50 caliber machine gun in lieu of the .30 caliber previously used. A second .50 caliber machine gun was mounted in the radio compartment. The single-socket nose gun socket was replaced with three machine gun sockets, one on each side of the nose above the bomb aiming panel, and one below and to the side of the bomb aiming panel.

Also new with the B-17C, and critical to the Flying Fortress's rugged reputation, was the incorporation of armor protection for the crew and critical systems. All of these changes made the aircraft heavier. To cope with the added weight, the B-17C featured more powerful versions of the R-1820 9-cylinder radial engine, the -65 model, which boasted 1,200 horsepower. Known as the B-17C to the USAAC, 20 of the aircraft were transferred to the British, who dubbed it Fortress I, and as such it saw its first combat on 8 July 1941. The remaining 18 aircraft in U.S. inventory were later updated to B-17D standards, and designated RB-17D (R for restricted use).

The Army Air Corps accepted 38 B-17Cs, which first flew in late July 1940 and entered service the following month. Crew armor and a crew oxygen system were added, as was an improved fuel system. The ventral machine gun mount allowed for only rearward firing of the weapon, and the angle of fire was limited. The gunner had to kneel in an awkward position in the tub in order to manually operate the guns. (Air Force Historical Research Agency)

This B-17C was photographed at Wright Field, Ohio, shortly after entering the service on 15 October 1940. Visible under the nose is the RDF "football" antenna. Pitot-tube masts protrude diagonally from both sides of the nose below the cheek windows. The turbo-supercharged Wright 1820-65 Cyclone engines could develop 1,200 horsepower each. Two socket mounts for machine guns were installed in the clear nose. (National Museum of the United States Air Force)

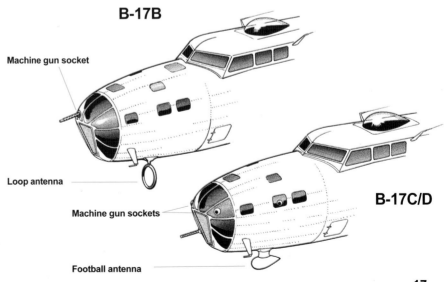

Nose Development

B-17B

Machine gun socket

Loop antenna

Machine gun sockets

B-17C/D

Football antenna

A flight of early B-17s, evidently -C models, soars past a mountain range with what appears to be a C-47 bringing up the rear. The army originally ordered 80 B-17Cs, but Boeing delivered only 38. The first 20 aircraft were transferred under Lend-Lease to Britain, where they were designated the Fortress I. The remaining 18 B-17Cs were ultimately upgraded to B-17D standards (primarily, with the addition of cowl flaps). (Air Force Historical Research Agency)

Although this aircraft has been identified in print as a B-17D, it lacks cowl flaps and is more likely a B-17C. The clear panels enclosing the radio operator's dorsal gun mount are somewhat visible: between the fixed front Plexiglas panel and the movable rear panel was a wind deflector, shown in the lowered position. Curiously, the red circle has been painted out of the national insignia on the wing but not on the insignia on the fuselage. (National Museum of the United States Air Force)

This B-17B, serial number 38-215 and nicknamed *Old Seventy,* was detailed to the Army Cold Weather Test Detachment, Ladd Field, Alaska, in early 1940 to perform flying tests in arctic conditions. A B-17C-type waist window is in evidence in the photo. *Old Seventy* performed patrol and bombing missions with the 36th Bomb Squadron during the Japanese invasion of the Aleutians, and crashed with no survivors on 18 July 1942. (National Museum of the United States Air Force)

Armament Development

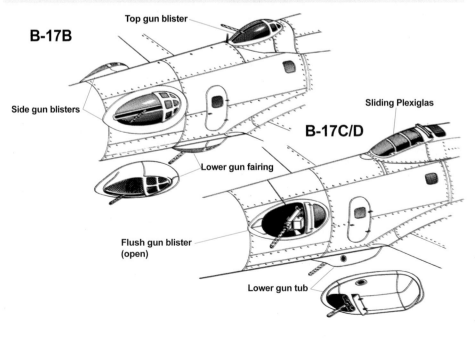

B-17B

Top gun blister

Side gun blisters

Lower gun fairing

Flush gun blister (open)

Sliding Plexiglas

B-17C/D

Lower gun tub

A B-17C soars above a coastline. It is painted Olive Drab on the upper surfaces and Neutral Gray on its underside; the tops of the cowls appear to be a dark green. The national star insignia still has the red circle in the center that was discontinued in May 1942. Immediately aft of the closest cowl is an air scoop. This scoop was not repeated on the inboard engine nacelles. There is a clear view of the engine exhaust on the inboard nacelle, where it bypasses the main landing gear well. Below the fuselage, aft of the ventral gun tub, is the marker beacon antenna, a wire antenna stretched between two short masts. Barely visible is the red hubcap on the main landing wheel. Fine oil streaks have spread out from the rears of the cowls. Painted on the tail in black is the number 2B, which indicates the 2nd Bomb Group. (Stan Piet collection)

The B-17D was in effect a slightly modified version of the B-17C, the principal difference being the addition of cowl flaps. The Army Air Corps received 42 B-17Ds, with the serial number range 40-3059 to 40-3100. In addition, 18 B-17Cs were upgraded to B-17D standards. Like the B-17C, the -D model had Wright R-1820-65 turbo-supercharged engines. This example was photographed on 3 February 1941. (National Museum of the United States Air Force)

The British began limited combat use of the B-17C on 8 July 1941. Their experiences highlighted deficiencies in the aircraft's design, and in response, changes were stipulated for the final 42 aircraft on the contract. The changes were so numerous and significant, however, that a new model designation was applied to the affected planes. Externally, the B-17D differed from the C by the addition of cowl flaps. Perhaps more significant was an unseen internal change – the inclusion of self-sealing fuel tanks. At the same time the electrical system was changed from 12- to 24-volt, a low-pressure oxygen system was added, and the bomb racks and release mechanisms were redesigned. Many of these changes were retrofitted to older B-17C aircraft as well. Another crew position was also added to the aircraft, which raised the total to 10. Deliveries of the B-17D began on 3 February 1941 and ran through 29 April 1941.

Seeing trouble brewing in the Pacific, the US Army Air Force, as the Army Air Corps had been renamed on 20 June 1941, transferred the bulk of the B-17Ds, with the 19th Bomb Group, to the Philippines during November 1941. Despite 4 December 1941 orders that the B-17s were to be moved to Del Monte Field on Mindanao, and thus out of Japanese range, the Japanese attackers on 8 December 1941 (local time) found half of the Flying Fortresses still at Clark Field, the Philippines. Out of the two squadrons on the ground at Clark at the time, only one of the bombers survived the Japanese assault.

The cowl flaps are closed on this B-17D. Other new features on the B-17D included augmented armor, twin machine guns in the dorsal and ventral mounts, self-sealing fuel tanks, and an improved electrical system. A round porthole was included on each side of the ventral gun tub. The aircraft commander's observation blister, which had been introduced on the B-17B, remained but, beginning with the -C model, it was moved to the aircraft's centerline. (National Museum of the United States Air Force)

The B-17D had two machine-gun sockets in the clear nose. Similar sockets were set into one cheek window on each side of the aircraft (the front window on the right side and the center window on the left), as well as into the front center overhead window in the bombardier's/navigator's compartment. The "football" RDF antenna was located slightly to the left of the centerline of the aircraft below the bombardier's compartment. (National Museum of the United States Air Force)

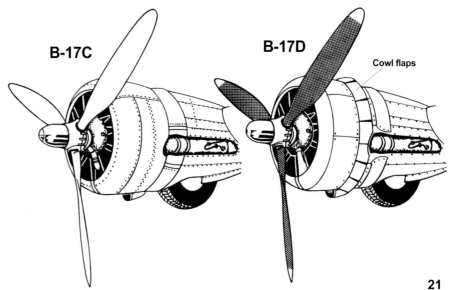

Cowl Development

B-17C

B-17D

Cowl flaps

Three B-17Ds sit on an airfield. The second aircraft wears the tail number 40/5B. Details visible on the closer aircraft include the fabric covers over the pitot tubes on either side of the nose; the engine exhaust on the inboard nacelle; the socket mounts for machine guns in the nose and the cheek window; the open cowl flaps; and the commander's observation blister and its opening at the center of the upper deck to the rear of the cockpit. (National Museum of the United States Air Force)

The same modified B-17D is seen from the front left. The center cheek window appears to lack the socket mount for a machine gun that was normally installed in this spot. The "football" housing for the RDF antenna is similarly missing from the fuselage below the bombardier's/navigator's compartment. (DAABMA)

This B-17D exhibits several modifications. The ventral gun tub has been removed and faired over. A clear nose that is definitely not a B-17D type has been installed; it lacks the metal framing of the B-17D-style nose, and may have been a B-17F nose unit. A coat of matte black has been applied on the undersides of the aircraft, evidently for night camouflage. Paint appears to have been roughly applied over a tail number. (DAABMA)

After receiving her new tail, B-17D 40-3097 was renamed *The Swoose*. No longer combat worthy, it served as the personal transport of General George Brett. Scheduled to be broken up at Kingman Air Base after the war, it was saved through the efforts of one of her former pilots, George Kurtz. Long stored at the National Air & Space Museum's Paul Garber Facility, *The Swoose* moved to the U.S. Air Force Museum in 2008. (DAABMA)

The B-17E, the first of which is shown here, represents a major reworking of the Flying Fortress. An enlarged and reshaped tail section has been installed, and there is a twin-.50-caliber machine gun emplacement in the tail. The fuselage to the rear of the wings was enlarged to accommodate the new tail and gun mount. A Sperry A1 turret with twin .50-caliber machine guns aft of the cockpit provided greatly increased defensive protection. (Air Force Historical Research Agency)

Boeing and the Army Air Force had been taught a brutal lesson at the hands of Germans and Japanese and the B-17 was heavily redesigned based on these experiences. The new design was designated B-17E, and was assigned the Boeing model number 299-O. Boeing would use the same model number for the subsequent F and G models. Virtually the entire fuselage from the cockpit aft was new. The enlarged fuselage incorporated a rear gunner's position fitted with twin .50-caliber machine guns, improved waist gun positions; each armed with a .50-caliber machine gun; a Sperry A-1 top turret, sporting twin .50-caliber machine guns mounted just behind the pilot's and copilot's seats, and a remote-control Sperry number 645705-D turret (again, with twin .50-caliber machine guns) replacing the previous belly "bathtub" position. Atop all of this was a completely new vertical stabilizer that dwarfed the unit previously used, and completely altered the profile of the aircraft. All of these changes increased the weight of the aircraft by 2,500 pounds (the A-1 top turret alone weighing 700 pounds). But careful design meant that the top speed only dropped six miles per hour despite use of the same R-1820-65 powerplants as in its predecessor. Cruising speed fell a mere one mile per hour.

Ventral Development

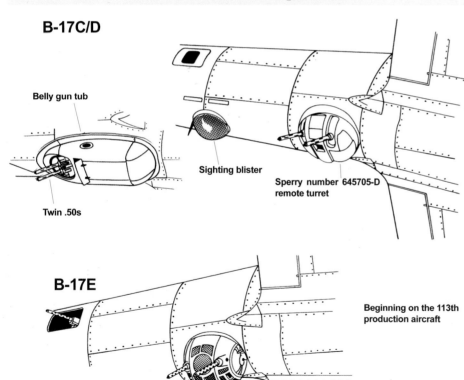

B-17C/D

Belly gun tub

Sighting blister

Sperry number 645705-D remote turret

Twin .50s

B-17E

Beginning on the 113th production aircraft

Sperry ball turret

Factory workers look on as the first B-17E, serial number 41-2393, runs up her engines during tests on a hardstand at the Boeing plant. The Army Air Corps issued Boeing the contract for the B-17E on 30 August 1940, and this aircraft made its maiden flight on 5 September 1941. As with the B-17C and B-17D, the engines on the B-17E remained the Wright R-1820-65 Cyclones, rated at 1,200 horsepower each. (DAABMA)

Another modification of the B-17E was the elimination of the ventral gun tub in favor of a remote-controlled Sperry number 645705-D turret with twin .50-caliber machine guns. A gunner remotely operated this turret using a periscopic sight in a clear dome aft of the turret, visible to the far right of this photo. This was not a good arrangement, as the gunner's position was awkward and numerous gunners suffered vertigo from operating the periscopic gun sight. (DAABMA)

The number-one B-17E in flight displays its unarmed Sperry number 645705-D ventral turret and the Plexiglas dome for the gunner's periscopic sight on the bottom of the fuselage. Two other new features are in view: the revamped sliding panel with a Plexiglas window at each waist machine gun position, and, further aft, the new rear entry/exit door with a small window. The waist machine guns were now installed on pedestal mounts. (Air Force Historical Research Agency)

The first B-17E warms up its engines. In addition to the two sockets for machine guns in the front center of the clear Plexiglas nose, with this model of Flying Fortress a third socket was added toward the lower right of the nose, as viewed from inside the aircraft. Sockets for additional machine guns remained in the center left cheek window and the front right cheek window. A trapezoidal bomb-aiming window and an RDF "football" are visible. (DAABMA)

An early B-17E displays U.S. Army markings and a national star with red circle on the undersides of its wings. The red circle on the fuselage insignia has been painted over with white. The paint scheme was Olive Drab on the upper surfaces and Neutral Gray on the lower ones. Matte black deicer boots, which prevented ice buildup on the wings, have been fitted on the leading edges of the wing, the vertical tail, and the stabilizers. (National Museum of the United States Air Force)

This B-17E, reportedly with the 5th Bomb Group, 72d Bomb Squadron, was photographed on Eastern Island, Midway, in late May or early June 1942. Director John Ford's documentary film, *The Battle of Midway*, contains a glimpse of this aircraft taken at the same time. There are at least three different colors on the aircraft's upper surfaces. The bare-metal cowl flaps evidently indicate that they were replaced after the aircraft was painted. (DAABMA)

The Sperry ball turret was an important improvement over the awkward-to-operate remote-controlled Sperry number 645705-D turret installed in the first 112 B-17Es. Enclosed in the Sperry turret, the gunner moved in unison with the guns, greatly improving his combat-effectiveness. Here, Staff Sergeant Donald Herman of Canton, Ohio, sits curled up inside his ball turret. There is very little clearance between the bottom of the turret and the ground. (National Archives)

Shown making a practice bombing run with its bomb-bay doors open is a ball-turret-equipped B-17E, serial number 41-2567. Painted in black on the undersides of the wings was "U.S. Army." Exhaust streaking is prominent under the wings. This Flying Fortress never made it out of the States; mechanical failure brought its career to an end at Rosecrans Field, near St. Joseph, Missouri, in October 1942, with the loss of three crewmen. (Stan Piet collection)

The B-17E was the first version of the Flying Fortress that Boeing mass produced, and the company experienced some growing pains in securing adequate parts and subcomponents from its vendors. Exacerbating the problem was the fact that B-17E production coincided with the United States' concerted drive to rapidly place itself on a war footing. Boeing delivered 512 B-17Es to the U.S. Army. (Air Force Historical Research Agency)

B-17E serial number 41-2600 bears her nickname, *Esmeralda,* in yellow script letters below the cheek windows. The B-17E was the first model of the Flying Fortress to have a fully retracting tail wheel; this design measure was intended to partially offset the increased drag caused by the dorsal turret. The main landing gear wheels still partially extended below the engine nacelles when fully retracted. (Air Force Historical Research Agency)

A B-17E at an unidentified airfield displays a relatively fresh-appearing camouflage paint job, but the propellers appear to have seen considerable wear, as much of the matte black paint has peeled off the surfaces. The square inlet on the leading edge of the wing next to the inboard engine nacelle is the oil cooler intake. The recessed landing light is also visible on the leading edge of the wing. This aircraft mounts the Sperry 645705-D ventral turret. (Stan Piet collection)

Mechanics work on the engines of B-17E serial number 41-9023, nicknamed *Yankee Doodle,* at Grafton Underwood Airfield, near Kettering in Northamptonshire, England, on 9 June 1942. A little over a month later, this Flying Fortress took part in the first bombing raid conducted by the VIII Bomber Command, against Rouen, France, and Brigadier General Ira Eaker, commander of the VIII, flew aboard *Yankee Doodle.* The aircraft bore an RAF camouflage scheme at this time. (Air Force Historical Research Agency)

B-17E serial number 41-2504, attached to the VI Air Force, flies at low altitude over the Panama Canal Zone. The unusual camouflage scheme appears to have been achieved by applying light gray paint over parts of the Olive Drab upper side surfaces in splotchy patterns. The bomber is outfitted for antisubmarine patrol work, as indicated by the ASV (air-to-surface-vessel) radar antennas on the nose and under the wing. (National Museum of the United States Air Force)

Tugboat Annie was the nickname of this B-17E, serial number 41-2599, shown flying over mountainous terrain probably in the U.S. Pacific Northwest before being deployed overseas. She served in the Southwest Pacific successively with the 19th and 43rd Bomb Groups and participated in the sinking of the Japanese destroyer *Yayoi* in September 1942. *Tugboat Annie* was ditched close to the southeastern shore of New Guinea between the towns of Lae and Buna, on 16 January 1943. (Stan Piet collection)

Several major improvements of the B-17E over preceding models are visible in this photo. The enlarged vertical stabilizer and rudder improved the stability of the Flying Fortress, while the tail turret provided potent defensive fire to the rear of the aircraft. The tail gunner knelt in his compartment below a tightly fitting clear enclosure, with a bicycle seat to rest on, and aimed and fired the guns with his hands directly on their grips. (National Museum of the United States Air Force)

A ground crewman prepares to pass a yellow practice bomb to an armorer inside the bomb bay of a B-17E. Two types of practice bombs are on the bomb trailer in the foreground. There is a red caution flag to the front of the trailer bed. The four vertical cylinders on top of the front of the trailer were storage brackets for the bomb fins, which normally were installed on the bombs after they were attached to the bomb racks. (Stan Piet collection)

Two B-17Es, serial numbers 41-9141 and 41-9131, were photographed sometime before mid-1942. While the Flying Fortress in the background has Olive Drab upper surfaces, the nearer bomber has an RAF high-altitude, daylight-bombing camouflage scheme of Dark Green and Dark Earth on the upper surfaces and Azure Blue on the lower surfaces. An RAF-style tricolor recognition flash is painted on the tail. The closer aircraft, serial number 41-9141, displays the RAF camouflage scheme for high-altitude daylight bombers. There is a clearly defined, straight demarcation between the upper and lower camouflage colors above the cheek windows. The RAF acquired 45 B-17Es in mid-1942, redesignating them the Fortress IIA, but records indicate 41-9141 never served with the RAF. (Air Force Historical Research Agency)

This B-17E, serial number 41-2656, had the nickname *Chief Seattle* from the Pacific Northwest emblazoned on the front of the fuselage, in honor of the citizens of Seattle, Washington, who funded this aircraft through a bond drive. After its christening on 5 March 1942, *Chief Seattle* served in the Pacific Theater and was attached to the 19th Bomb Group when it was lost while flying a patrol on 14 August 1942. (Air Force Historical Research Agency)

Three crewmen take a milk and sandwich break in the waist gunners' position of a B-17E. At this stage of the B-17's development, the .50-caliber waist machine guns were on pintle mounts atop vertical pedestals braced to the fuselage frame. Ammunition trays were attached to the mounts. In the background is the rear bulkhead of the radio compartment. (Stan Piet collection)

Esmeralda's tail machine gun position, dorsal turret, and the ball turret are equipped with their .50-caliber machine guns in this slightly closer view of the aircraft that also appears on page 28. Faintly visible on the roof of the cockpit above the copilot is a window. Two Plexiglas roof windows, one each above the pilot's and copilot's seats, were installed beginning with the B-17E model. (Air Force Historical Research Agency)

Two waist gunners equipped with oxygen masks demonstrate the operation of their .50-caliber machine guns, which are configured to receive ammunition via belts from the plywood boxes in the background. The waist guns in the B-17E (and other B-17 models up to late examples of the B-17G) were directly across from each other. Thus, the gunners had to contend with getting in each other's way when the action became hot. (Air Force Historical Research Agency)

Suzy Q, B-17E serial number 41-2489 of the 19th Bomb Group, 93rd Bomb Squadron, had her dorsal turret removed when photographed on a hardstand in Australia. Her name was written above the cheek windows instead of the apparently more common position for nicknames below these windows. *Suzy Q* became one of the most famous B-17s of the war, owing to a feature article on her in the 18 January 1943, issue of *Life* magazine. (National Museum of the United States Air Force)

B-17E serial number 41-9205 suffered a ground accident with no crew injuries at Fort Glenn, Alaska, on 4 December 1942, when its right main landing gear brake failed while taxiing in strong crosswinds. Less than a year after the bomber was repaired and returned to service, her pilot, Irwin K. McWilliams, ditched her into Lake Bennett, Yukon Territory, on 16 October 1943, resulting in the deaths of five crewmen. (National Museum of the United States Air Force)

Crewmen pose next to *Typhoon McGoon II,* a B-17E, serial number 41-9211, with the 11th Bomb Group, 98th Bomb Squadron, on New Caledonia in January 1943. This Flying Fortress patrolled the sea lanes and took part in bombing missions in the Southwest Pacific area. Protruding from her clear nose is one of the antennas of the ASV radar array. There also was an ASV antenna under each wing. (National Museum of the United States Air Force)

B-17E serial number 41-9131 wears early-war markings, with the red circles in the national insignia evidently painted out on the fuselage and still intact on the wing. The aircraft is in relatively clean condition, with just some light exhaust smudging behind the superchargers. The excellent fit of the fuselage panels of the Flying Fortresses is apparent, including the precision fit of the bomb bay doors. (National Museum of the United States Air Force)

This aircraft has an extra socket mount, next to the center of the clear nose, in which the .50-caliber machine gun is inserted. Inside the Plexiglas to the left is a brace from the central socket to the airframe. Adjacent to the lower machine gun socket (lower left) is a hinged access panel. Retrospectively, its not clear if the weight of the extra machine gun, FlaK or debris cracked the bomb-aiming window. (Air Force Historical Research Agency)

A bombardier operates the .50-caliber machine gun in the center socket of a B-17E. Four tubular braces around the socket, along with the buffered cradle the gun is mounted in, helped absorb the heavy pounding of the weapon when firing. The right socket is taped shut to exclude wind. Above the bombardier's head is an adjustable lamp. The round object tucked into the aircraft's frame at the top left is a navigational computer. (Air Force Historical Research Agency)

B-17E serial number 41-9100, *Birmingham Blitzkrieg,* was relegated to a formation aircraft after the 379th Bomb Group, 525th Bomb Squadron, transitioned to the B-17F. Photographed in July 1944, she wore matte red and white stripes, making her more visible as she helped other bombers assemble in formation before advancing to the Continent. Both the dorsal and ball turrets have been removed and faired over. (National Museum of the United States Air Force)

This B-17E, serial number 41-2629, was one of the early Flying Fortresses to serve in England with the 97th Bomb Group, but by the time this series of photographs was taken, she bore the squadron markings of the 92nd Bomb Group, 326th Bomb Squadron. The hubcap of the main wheel bore a distinctive design: a white Star of David on a dark background. An enlarged center window had been installed in the cheek. (Stan Piet collection)

Alabama Exterminator II, a B-17E, serial number 41-9022, served successively with the 97th, 92nd, and 384th Bomb Groups from 1942 to 1943. She appears as she did when she was relegated to a target-tow and liaison aircraft, shorn of her dorsal and ball turrets. She still bears the "PY" unit code for the 407th Bomb Squadron, 92nd Bomb Group. At some point in her career, a nose from a B-17F replaced her original nose. This change was found on other aircraft as well. (Stan Piet collection)

The nose of *Alabama Exterminator II* is shown in close-up. The aircraft's nomenclature, serial number, and crew weight are faintly stenciled below the rear cheek window. Written on the RDF antenna housing is "Holmes Bastard Bomber," a reference to Lieutenant John Holmes, pilot of Alabama Exterminator II while it was assigned to the 97th Bomb Group. Two sheet-metal patches are visible to the front of and above *Exterminator.* (Stan Piet collection)

B-17E, serial number 41-2629, takes off from Mount Farm (Station 234), north of Dorchester, Oxfordshire, while assigned to the 1st Combat Crew Replacement Center. This aircraft had a convoluted career, the 92nd Bomb Group having acquired it from the 305th Bomb Group in December 1942, and the 100th Bomb Group having received it from the 92nd in March 1943. Faintly visible on the ground in the left background is a row of P-38 Lightnings. (Stan Piet collection)

Rhett Butler, a B-17E nicknamed after the character in *Gone with the Wind,* exhibits the snubbed Plexiglas nose with metal frames that was a key identifying feature of that model. In the background is the model that succeeded the B-17E: the B-17F, which displays that model's new, frameless, and more prominent clear nose. Also visible on the B-17F are the tail and ball turrets. Both bombers have Sperry dorsal turrets. (Stan Piet collection)

As a precautionary measure should the demand for Wright Cyclone engines outweigh the supply, and in order to boost the performance of the Flying Fortress, Vega Aircraft Corporation, a subsidiary of Lockheed Aircraft Company, contracted with the USAAF in July 1942 to develop the experimental XB-38, featuring four Allison V-1710-89 V12 inline, liquid-cooled engines on the airframe of B-17E serial number 41-2401.

To achieve the conversion to the V-1710-89 engines on the XB-38, it was necessary to rework some external and internal features of the wings. To cool the engines, radiators were necessary, and these were installed in the leading edges of the wings between the engines, with large, rectangular air inlets to their fronts. Plumbing for the water-cooling system was installed inside each of the wings.

The engines of the XB-38 are warming up at Vega's Burbank plant. Each Allison V-1710-89 engine could generate 1,425 horsepower, 225 more horsepower than the Wright R-1820-65 engines of the B-17E. The XB-38 thus enjoyed 900 horsepower more than the B-17E. Below the propeller spinners on the fronts of the nacelles are air intakes for the oil coolers. The pitot tubes were moved up to new spots.

It is apparent that the engine nacelles and propeller spinners of the XB-38 extended noticeably farther to the front than the cowls and propellers of the B-17E. A rough mock-up of a Sperry ball turret was installed in place of the 645705-D ventral turret originally installed in the B-17E. The Plexiglas dome for the previously-used remote periscope sight remained in place on the underside of the fuselage aft of the star insignia.

Workers at the Vega plant in Burbank have gathered around the XB-38, the cowling panels of which have been removed from the number-one and -two engines, revealing the Allison V-1710-89 engines, engine mounts, oil coolers, and other mechanical components. The nacelles of the XB-38 were hand-built and reportedly were coated with aluminum paint. By May 1943 the aircraft was ready to be flight-tested.

Engines No. three and four of the XB-38 are shown with the cowling panels removed. On the undersides of the XB-38's engine nacelles, below the oil coolers, were retractable doors that acted as outlets for the oil-cooler air; these doors are shown fully open. Immediately aft of the closer propeller spinner is a scoop that admitted cooling air for the exhaust manifold. The tire tread pattern is also visible.

The XB-38's engines are warming up. The square openings below the leading edge of the wing to the left are, left to right, the engine supercharger ram air intake and the intercooler intake. There was a pair of such intakes for each engine. The small bulge at the lower rear of the cowl panel of the number-three engine acted to streamline the exposed front end of the exhaust line where it exited the engine compartment.

The streamlined, expertly fashioned engine nacelles and spinners of the XB-38 gave the stock B-17E a hot-rodded, sleek appearance. Special instruments were installed inside the aircraft for testing purposes. The XB-38 made its maiden flight on 19 May 1943; the pilot was Bud Martin and the copilot was George MacDonald. It subsequently made five more successful test flights, achieving a maximum speed of 327 miles per hour. (National Museum of the United States Air Force)

During her sixth test flight out of Burbank, on 16 June 1943, a fire broke out in the XB-38's number-three engine. Although the pilot, Bud Martin, activated that engine's fire extinguisher, the flames spread through the nacelle. Martin and his copilot, George MacDonald, bailed out, but Martin was killed in the fall and MacDonald critically injured. The XB-38 crashed in an unoccupied area and was destroyed. (National Museum of the United States Air Force)

First contracted for in 1941 and first flown in May 1942, the B-17F differed visually from the B-17E mainly in the new, all-Plexiglas nose, which extended farther to the front than that of the B-17E. Although Boeing produced 2,300 of the -F model, Douglas and Vega also manufactured, respectively, 605 and 500 of these bombers. *Snafu* was a Douglas-built B-17F-40-DL with the 94th Bomb Group, 332nd Bomb Squadron. (Stan Piet collection)

Aside from its new, frameless Plexiglas nose cone, the B-17F looked virtually identical to the B-17E on the outside. Internally, however, the B-17F was a much different aircraft. Over 400 items differed between the two models, including a new model of the Wright Cyclone engines, the R-1820-97, which at the War Emergency setting generated 1,380 horsepower. To harness the increased power more efficiently at altitude, new paddle-blade Hamilton Standard propellers were fitted, which required a modification to the design of the cowlings. These new propellers were also one inch larger in diameter. Inside the wing outer panels were now found fuel tanks – the so-called "Tokyo tanks" – that increased the aircraft's range to 4,220 miles. Beneath the wings were now found external bomb racks, which though rarely used, added 4,000 pounds to the aircraft's bomb capacity. Glide bomb attachments were installed at the factory on B-17F-1-VE and B-17F-10-DL aircraft.

In an effort to thwart frontal attacks, modification centers began installing cheek guns on the noses of some B-17Fs prior to their delivery to combat units. The cheek gun positions began to be installed at the factory, beginning with Boeing B-17F-55-BO (serial number 42-29467) and Douglas B-17F-15-DL (serial number 42-3004), and at a indeterminate point by Lockheed-Vega.

Even with the cheek guns, front defense was lacking, and beginning with B-17F-75-DL (serial number 42-3504), the Bendix chin turret began to be installed. Not only did the resultant aircraft strongly resemble the B-17Gs, they were so similar that the USAAF operationally considered them a B-17G, despite their builder's specifications.

Nose Cone Development

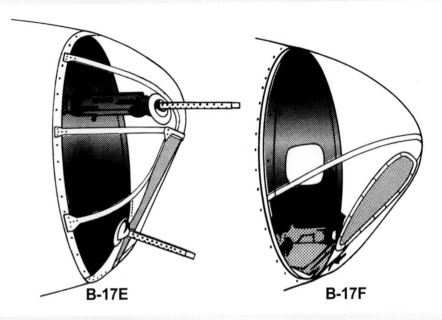

B-17E　　　　**B-17F**

Nose and Cheek Gun Development

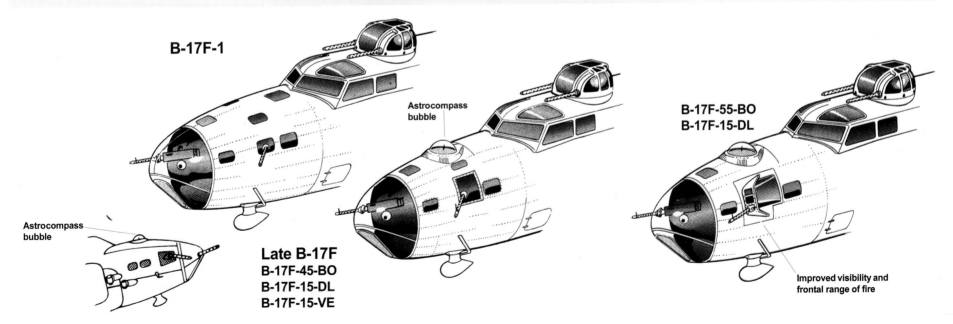

B-17F-1

Astrocompass
bubble

B-17F-55-BO
B-17F-15-DL

Astrocompass
bubble

Late B-17F
B-17F-45-BO
B-17F-15-DL
B-17F-15-VE

Improved visibility and
frontal range of fire

Although early B-17Fs had three windows of roughly equal size on each of the cheeks, during production a larger window was installed on each side at the cheek machine gun position. The larger cheek-gun window on this Vega B-17F is in an unusual position at the front of the fuselage, instead of in the more common center-window position. New, paddle-bladed Hamilton Standard propellers were installed on the B-17Fs. (National Archives)

Fittings for under-wing bomb racks were introduced to the B-17F during production. Armorers are loading two bombs on the racks of a B-17F at Framlingham (Station 153) in Suffolk, England, on 29 September 1943. Although the original caption to the photo asserted that the crew was loading glide bombs, the first U.S. glide bomb, the BG-1, was not used until the following year. These bombs were more likely 2,000-pound general-purpose (GP). (National Archives)

Although earlier models of the B-17 did see combat, the B-17F and later B-17G, truly carried the U.S. war effort into Europe. While ultimately Allied air power virtually swept the Luftwaffe from the skies, FlaK remained a threat for the duration of the conflict. Bomb-bay doors open and enveloped in moderately heavy FlaK, a B-17G begins a bomb run. The C in the square on the tail indicates that this Flying Fortress was with the 96th Bomb Group. (National Museum of the United States Air Force)

This Douglas-built B-17F-30-DL, serial number 42-3172, was dubbed *Miss Patricia* when it briefly served with the 306th Bomb Group. Reassigned to 91st Bomb Group, 323rd Bomb Squadron, Bassingbourn (Station 121), in Cambridgeshire, England, she had been renamed *Chennault's Pappy* when photographed on 9 April 1944. Bomb trailers with an interesting assortment of ordnance stand by, ready to replenish the bombers. (National Archives)

Crewmen load light-blue practice bombs into *Damifino,* a B-17F. The upper half of the aircraft's clear nose is joined to a multi-section lower half, in the front center of which is the optically flat bomb-aiming window. What appears to be dark green paint has been sprayed over the Olive Drab next to the cockpit, but the dark streak on the fuselage aft of the painted nickname seems to be the propeller's shadow. (Stan Piet collection)

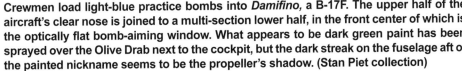

Armorers install .50-caliber machine gun barrel units into the guns' receivers in a B-17F ball turret. There were removable panels in the rear of the turret for just this purpose. To prevent corrosion and facilitate maintenance, all of the defensive guns' barrels were usually removed from the weapons when the aircraft was on the ground. The gunner's access hatch is open, revealing its prominent "NO STEP" stencil. (Stan Piet collection)

Redmond Annie, this B-17F's nickname, may have referred to the Redmond, Oregon, army airfield. Above the nickname is a painting of a woman on a mule lassoing an airplane. It is unclear whether this photo was taken at Redmond. The bomber was undergoing refueling from the tanker truck at the left. The fourth man from left has casually slung a shearling flight jacket over his shoulder. (Stan Piet collection)

From left to right, Sergeants Edward Casaceli and Kenneth Finnegan, Corporal Edward Weber, and Sergeant Joseph LaBarbera load ammunition for the Browning twin-.50-caliber machine guns of a Sperry ball turret in a B-17F in North Africa. At first, ammunition was stored inside the ball turret, as here, but in later turrets the ammo was stored in boxes mounted on the supporting structure above the turret. (National Archives)

Mechanics have removed the left main landing gear wheel from a B-17F, perhaps for performing maintenance on the brake. To the right is a yellow jack stand, supporting the left side of the aircraft during the operation. The propeller has been removed from the number-two engine, which is also undergoing work. To the side of the second man from left is a light-duty scaffolding, commonly used by ground crews working on bombers. (Stan Piet collection)

Two crewmen inspect a B-17 main landing gear tire that was riddled by FlaK during a raid on Naples Harbor in Italy on 4 April 1943. The damaged tire made for a rough but successful landing. This was the first raid on the Continent by the Northwest African Air Forces, and all of the nearly 100 bombers that participated in the mission returned safely to base, even though escort fighters had not accompanied them. (National Archives)

Mechanics replace an engine on *Werewolf,* a B-17F-27-BO, serial number 41-24606, with the 303rd Bomb Group, 358th Bomb Squadron, on the grounds of a mental hospital at Dawlish, Devon, England, where the pilot, First Lieutenant George L. Oxrider, had made an emergency landing on 23 January 1943. The VIII Service Command Mobile Repair Unit finished the repairs by April 22. (National Museum of the United States Air Force)

Arguably the most famous aircraft of World War II, the *Memphis Belle* was Boeing B-17F-10-BO serial number 41-24485. Based at Bassingbourn, in Cambridgeshire, England, with the 324th Bomb Squadron, she was the first U.S. heavy bomber to complete 25 missions. Subsequently, she and her crew returned to the United States on a public-relations tour to help sell war bonds, and she was photographed at National Airport, Washington, D.C. (Stan Piet collection)

The left side of *Memphis Belle's* nose was photographed during her U.S. tour. Pilot Robert K. Morgan named her after the hometown of his girlfriend, Margaret Polk. The nose art was based on a pinup by George Petty in the April 1941 issue of *Esquire* magazine and was painted by Corporal Tony Starcer. The painted bombs represented the aircraft's 25 missions, and the eight swastikas stood for the German aircraft kills the crew claimed. (National Archives)

Lieutenant General Jacob Devers, commander of all U.S. Army forces in Europe, congratulates Captain Robert Morgan and the rest of the crew of the *Memphis Belle* before their departure for the United States from Bovingdon, in Hertfordshire, England, on 9 June 1943. Morgan and the second crewman from left are wearing Pattern 41 flying boots procured from the RAF, while the other crewmen are wearing U.S. A6 flying boots. (National Archives)

The artwork on the *Memphis Belle* was not uniform. The bathing suit was blue on the left side of the aircraft, and red on the right. Also, individual crew members' stations were marked.

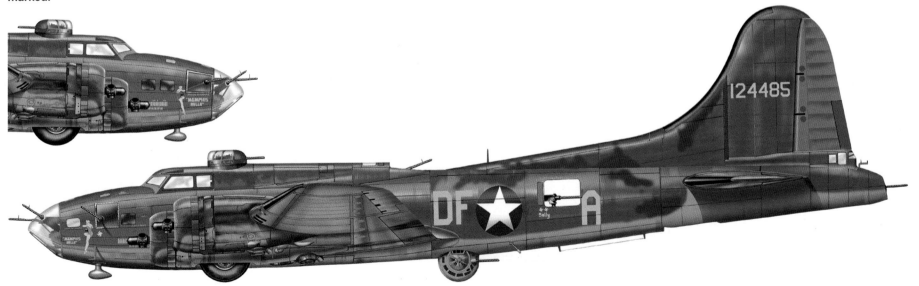

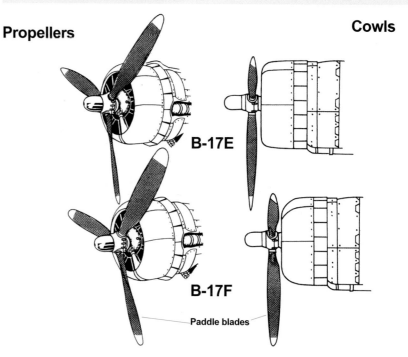

Propeller and Cowl Developments

Propellers

Cowls

B-17E

B-17F

Paddle blades

This aggregation of USAAF aircraft on a flight line at Patterson Field, Ohio, may have been part of a wartime display. In the foreground is a Douglas-manufactured B-17F-40-DL, serial number 42-3236, wearing what appears to have been a mottled gray and green camouflage. Atop the fuselage to the front of the cockpit is an astrodome, which was installed on the Douglas Flying Fortresses starting with the B-17F-15-DL model. (Stan Piet collection)

Knock Out Dropper, B-17F-27-BO 41-24605 was the first B-17 to complete 50, and later 75, missions in Europe. She flew with the 359th Bomb Squadron, 303rd Bomb Group out of Molesworth, in Cambridgeshire, England. The aircraft was scrapped at Stillwater, Oklahoma, in July 1945.

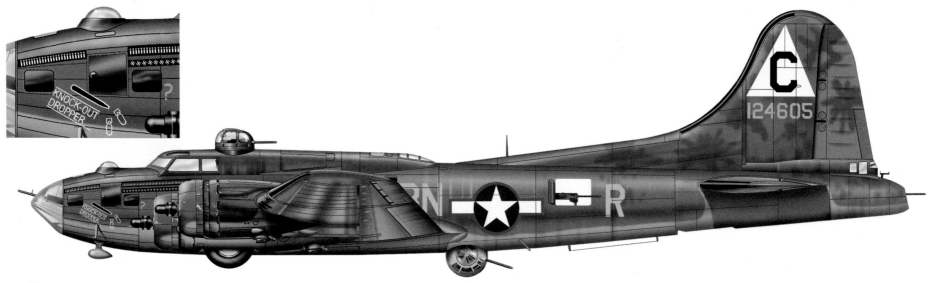

A Boeing B-17F-95-BO, serial number 42-30243, cruises at altitude, displaying her underwing bomb racks. These racks, each of which had a 2,000-pound capacity, were introduced with the Boeing B-17F-30-BO, Douglas B-17F-20-DL, and Vega B-17F-20-VE models. Experience showed that the external racks had undesirable effects on aircraft performance, and eventually they were discontinued. (Air Force Historical Research Agency)

Miss Barbara, a B-17F-20-BO, serial number 41-24519, rests on a tarmac during World War II. This aircraft was delivered to Wright Field on 28 July 1942, and spent the war at various stateside bases and assignments, including a stint with Material Command at Wright Field in October 1942. Her last known assignment was in a glider test program at Vandalia, Ohio, in August 1943. (Stan Piet collection)

The Mud Hen is a B-17F fitted out for long-range photo-reconnaissance and/or mission-recording work with the addition of several optically flat camera windows in the bombardier's compartment. The national insignia appearing here on the fuselage displays the red border in use during the brief time frame of June to August 1943. On the tail is an RAF-style tricolor recognition flash. The ball turret has been removed and faired over. (Stan Piet collection)

Three B-17Fs from the 91st Bomb Group fly in formation. The two Flying Fortresses in the foreground and to the left bear the "LL" code of the 401st Bomb Squadron. In the foreground, with a mottled camouflage scheme, is *Royal Flush,* serial number 42-5132. The bomber in the right background, 42-3213, was assigned to the 323rd Bomb Squadron, 91st Bomb Group, when it ditched in the English Channel on 16 August 1943. (Stan Piet collection)

A close-up of *The Mud Hen* displays the humorous nose art. Casting a shadow across the hen's extended leg is the left pitot-tube mast. Two of the camera windows are visible: one below the forward cheek window, and another on the underside of the fuselage to the front of the RDF "football" antenna. There are protective wrappings around the barrels of the machine guns mounted in the sockets in the nose. (Stan Piet)

Thunderbird, a Boeing B-17F-105-BO, serial number 42-30453, of the 94th Bomb Group, 333rd Bomb Squadron, lifts off from Bury St. Edmunds (Station 468), Suffolk, England, in 1943. This photo was probably taken very shortly before the bomber went down during a mission to Regensburg in August 1943, since the red border around the national insignia, discontinued that month, has been painted over in blue. (Stan Piet collection)

The pilot of *The Careful Virgin* makes a low pass over the field in June 1943, celebrating his completion of 25 missions. At this time, air crew completing 25 missions were relieved of further combat duty, and such maneuvers by jubilant men, although against regulations, were largely tolerated. On the tail is the unit symbol of the 91st Bomb Group: a black letter *A* within a white triangle. In the foreground is an extremely rare decontamination vehicle based on a GMC CCKW chassis, while in front of it is a Diamond T 4-ton wrecker. (National Museum of the United States Air Force)

Flying Fortresses from the 401st Bomb Squadron, 91st Bomb Group, Bassingbourn (Station 121), Cambridgeshire, England, fly in formation. In the foreground is a B-17F-60-BO, serial number 42-29536, dubbed *Mary Ruth / Memories of Mobile.* Her pilot, First Lieutenant Loren E. Roll, named her after Mary Ruth King, whom he had met and married in Mobile, Alabama, in March 1943 while 42-29536 was undergoing engine replacement there. (National Archives)

The Careful Virgin, B-17F 41-24639, was the last of the first 300 B-17F models built by Boeing, and one of the first nine aircraft assigned to the 323rd Bomb Squadron of the 91st Bomb Group. The aircraft completed 80 combat missions over Germany before being transferred to the Air Force Service Command. Next assigned to Project Aphrodite, the aircraft became a flying bomb. Here, in happier days, she buzzes the tower at Bassingbourn. (National Museum of the United States Air Force)

Two Flying Fortresses from the 91st Bomb Group, 322nd Bomb Squadron, proceed on a mission. Both bear the squadron code "LG," and the individual aircraft letters, O and P, appear aft of the waist windows. In the foreground is *Mizpah, the Bearded Beauty,* a B-17F-10-BO serial number 41-24453 with mottled camouflage. It was shot down on the Schweinfurt raid of 17 August 1943, with the loss of five crewmen. (National Archives)

The 97th Bomb Group in North Africa used this combat-damaged B-17F for training aircrews in aircraft-ditching techniques. Members of the 414th Bomb Squadron practice escaping the aircraft and deploying the inflatable raft. The open compartment for stowing the raft is to the center of the photo. There was a life-raft compartment on each side. The doors to these compartments could be opened from inside the fuselage. (National Archives)

The skin has peeled off the side of this B-17 where it was hit in combat. It is possible that the damage was caused by a cannon round from a German fighter, since there also appears to be a puncture from a machine gun round in the star in the national insignia. The white of the star has been subdued with a darker color to make it less visible. The border of the insignia presumably was yellow, as used in the North African theater. (National Museum of the United States Air Force)

A direct hit severely damaged this B-17F, blowing a sizeable section out of the side of the fuselage aft of the pilot's seat, and exposing the inner substructure of the dorsal turret. Directly underneath the external part of the turret is the ring mount, with oval lightening holes around it. Visible below the mount is the left turret support stanchion, to the inner side of which is the left ammunition box. The side window has been shattered. (National Museum of the United States Air Force)

At Great Ashfield Air Base in Suffolk, England, on 11 December 1943, this B-17F-115-BO, serial number 42-30651, lost its vertical tail when the wing of another bomber sliced into it in a taxiing accident. The plane was attached to the 385th Bomb Group, 551st Bomb Squadron. At the upper right, lying on the wing of the other bomber, is the severed tail, complete with the G-in-a-square unit symbol of the 385th Bomb Group and "065" from the serial number. (National Museum of the United States Air Force)

At Thorpe Abbotts (Station 139), in Norfolk, England, on 27 December 1943, a taxiing accident took place involving three Flying Fortresses: *King Bee,* a B-17F-65-DL, serial number 42-3474; B-17F-45-VE serial number 42-6094; and B-17G-10-DL number 42-37772. Under the wing of the B-17 to the left is the rear section of *King Bee,* with the rear of the radio compartment visible. The front section of *King Bee* is to the right. (National Museum of the United States Air Force)

The crash scene at Thorpe Abbotts on 27 December 1943 is seen here from another angle. Crewmen are spraying fire-retardant foam around the crash scene. The tail section of *King Bee* at the right displays a black D in a white circle, the unit symbol of the 100th Bomb Group. Wedged under the front fuselage of the *King Bee* to the left is a ground vehicle, the wheels of which are visible. Amazingly, no air crewmen died in this accident. (National Museum of the United States Air Force)

Oh Nausea! was a B-17F-85-BO, serial number 42-30042, with the 100th Bomb Group, 349th Bomb Squadron. Damaged during the Regensburg raid on 17 August 1943, the crew ditched the aircraft in the Mediterranean after a failed attempt to fly to North Africa. The Germans captured the entire crew. The bomber features an astrodome above the bombardier's and navigator's compartment. The astrodome was added beginning with B-17F-45-BO, B-17F-15-DL and B-17F-15-VE production. (Stan Piet collection)

In an iconic photo symbolizing the Flying Fortress' ability to endure incredible damage and still limp back to base, *All American,* a B-17F-5-BO, serial number 41-24406, with the 97th Bomb Group, 414th Bomb Squadron, displays a huge gash in her fuselage and empennage from a collision with a Messerschmitt Bf 109 over Tunisia on 1 February 1943. The left stabilizer and elevator were completely severed in the collision. (National Museum of the United States Air Force)

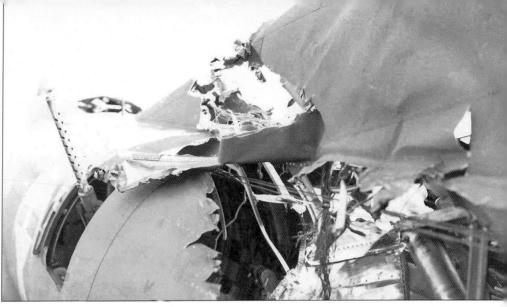

The pilot of *All American,* Lieutenant Kendrick R. Bragg, managed to fly her back to Biskrah, Algeria. Once on the ground, she was photographed from various angles and was inspected by technicians, including a Boeing field representative. Here, the area where the left stabilizer and elevator were sheared off is displayed along with the huge gash the Messerschmitt's wing sliced through the fuselage and front of the vertical tail. (National Museum of the United States Air Force)

The left side of the rear fuselage of *All American* aft of the waist gunner's window is shown close-up, with the rear landing gear shock absorber strut visible to the far right. Not long after the photo was taken, the vertical tail collapsed. Amazingly, *All American* was repaired and returned to service, being transferred to the 301st Bomb Group, 353rd Bomb Squadron, in March 1943, and after May 1943 serving as a squadron hack. (National Museum of the United States Air Force)

B-17F-35-DL serial number 42-3211 of the 381st Bomb Group, 535th Bomb Squadron, collided with a German fighter over the Continent on 14 July 1943, but was able to make its way back to England for a crash-landing at RAF Manston, in Kent. The roughly-painted *"T.S."* on the fuselage stood for *"Tough Shit."* The bomber was assigned squadron/aircraft code MS-O and wore the group's unit symbol of an L in a triangle. (Charles Bordner collection)

A ground crewman points to a hole inflicted by FW-190s in the windshield of *Tinker Toy,* B-17F-25-VE serial number 42-5846, 381st Bomb Group, 535th Bomb Squadron, on the 8 October 1943 mission to Bremen, Germany. The attack decapitated the pilot, First Lieutenant William Minerich, and wounded the copilot, who still managed to fly back to base. The aircraft was lost in a December 1943 return mission to Bremen. (Charles Bordner collection)

Sergeant Johnnie White painted the Bugs Bunny-themed art on *Wabbit Twacks III*, B-17F-85-BO serial number 42-30040 with the 96th Bomb Group, 337th Bomb Squadron. In this photograph the aircraft displays markings for 13 combat missions and 14 German fighters downed. *Wabbit Twacks III* was badly damaged during the 14 October 1943, raid on Schweinfurt, and all but one of the crew bailed out over France.

The nose art on *Ole Puss II* was another creation of the prolific Sergeant Johnnie White of the 96th Bomb Group. This B-17F-85-BO, serial number 42-30073, was assigned to the 413th Bomb Squadron, and should not be confused with another Fortress of the same bomb group, a B-17F-30-VE, serial number 42-5883, called *Ole Puss,* which sported similar nose art. *Ole Puss II's* career ended when it crash-landed on 17 April 1944.

First Lieutenant Thomas Paxton Sherwood of the 381st Bomb Group, 535th Bomb Squadron, stands next to a B-17F after returning from a bombing mission over Europe. He wears his officer's hat with the crown crumpled in the "fifty-mission crush" style. On 13 April 1944, with only a few more missions left before completing his tour of duty, Sherwood was shot down during a raid on the ball-bearing factory at Schweinfurt, Germany. Sherwood was captured and survived the ensuing year in a POW camp. (Sherwood family collection)

The XB-40/YB-40 program was a stopgap attempt to field a heavily armed escort aircraft to provide defensive firepower to bomber formations during long-range bombing missions until long-range fighter aircraft became available in quantity. Vega converted the prototype, designated the XB-40, from B-17F-1-BO serial number 41-34341. The idea was to greatly increase the number of machine guns of the aircraft, which would not carry a bomb load. The B-17F's dorsal, ball, and tail turrets were retained, the single guns in the waist positions were replaced by twin .50-caliber mounts, and a second dorsal turret with two .50-caliber machine guns replaced the radio operator's window-mounted single gun. Most striking of all, a remotely controlled turret was installed in the chin under the former location of the bombardier. The former bomb bay became an ammunition storage compartment. The XB-40 first flew in the fall of 1942, and the USAAF later took delivery of 20 service-test aircraft, designated YB-40 and based on B-17Fs, and four trainers, the TB-40, with Douglas Aircraft making the conversions at its Tulsa Modification Center. This YB-40, serial number 42-5927, was converted from a B-17F-35-VE. (Stan Piet collection)

Initially the upper rear deck of the fuselage of the XB-40 was faired into the front of the rear dorsal turret, for better streamlining. This extra dorsal turret was a Martin 250CE, the same model used on the B-24, B-26, A-20, and several other bombers. The ball turret is partially retracted: reportedly, the XB-40 was the only member of the B-17 family to have a retracting ball turret. YB-40s had the non-retractable ball turret.

In a view of the left side of the XB-40, the profile of the chin turret is visible. Designed by Bendix, the turret mounted two .50-caliber machine guns and was operated by a gunner sitting in the former bombardier's compartment in the nose. For streamlining, a fairing was added to the bottom of the fuselage immediately to the rear of the chin turret. A Bendix chin turret of a slightly different shape would become standard on the B-17G. (National Archives)

The prototype XB-40, with serial number 41-24341 on its tail, displays a modified, truncated fairing aft of the flight deck, eliminating the faired-in design of the rear dorsal turret. This new design allowed that turret to traverse fully, whereas the previous design limited traverse. Because of the space the rear dorsal turret consumed, there was no radioman in the XB-40/YB-40, communications duties being handled by the pilots. (National Archives)

The bottom of the Bendix chin turret in the XB-40 and YB-40 had a more symmetrical contour than that of the Bendix chin turret standardized in the B-17G, the lower front of which dipped down lower than the rear. The gun slots in the chin turret were continuous from the front to the rear, allowing clearance to the rears of the .50-caliber machine guns when these weapons were at maximum elevation, as seen in this photo.

The gun slots of the XB-40/YB-40 lacked the zippered covers found later on the chin turret of the B-17G. At the front of the turret is a Plexiglas access panel with an inspection window, useful when armorers were reloading or performing maintenance on the .50-caliber machine guns. Toward the top of the clear nose is the gun sight for the chin turret. Details of the joints in the various sections of the Plexiglas nose are visible.

Turret Developments

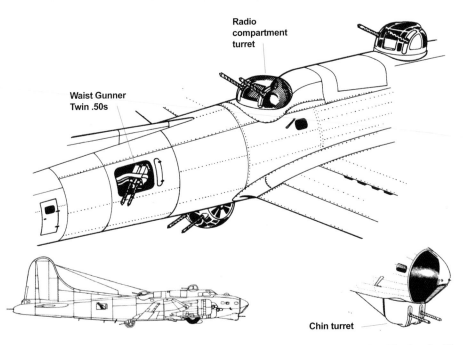

Radio compartment turret

Waist Gunner Twin .50s

Chin turret

The XB-40 displays the revised national insignia with side bars applied over the Mickey Mouse artwork. In combat, the YB-40 proved to be a less than ideal escort aircraft. It was not very maneuverable, so it was left to deal with enemy aircraft in a defensive rather than offensive capacity. And, when the escorted bombers had released their bomb loads and were racing home, the YB-40 would lag behind because of its great weight. (National Museum of the United States Air Force)

Resting on a snowy airfield is the XB-40. Twelve YB-40s were deployed to England with the 92nd Bomb Group at Alconbury (Station 102), in Cambridgeshire, and seven of these flew the first YB-40 combat mission to St.-Nazaire, on the Atlantic coast of France, on 27 May 1943. These tail-heavy aircraft struggled to keep up with B-17 formations and experienced problems with the ammunition-supply systems. The 92nd Group's brief experiment with the YB-40s ended in July 1943.

LET THEM COME GANG ILL TAKE CARE OF THEM!

Although the Bendix chin turret with twin .50-caliber machine guns was introduced on the last Douglas B-17Fs, this defensive feature became standard on the last model of the Flying Fortress, the B-17G. The first B-17G took to the air in May 1943, and a total of 8,680 of them were manufactured by Boeing, Douglas, and Vega. This B-17G-30-DL, serial number 42-38091, displayed an unusual variety of paint tones on its surfaces. (Stan Piet collection)

With 8,703 being produced, the B-17G was by far the most common version of the Flying Fortress. For many, the distinguishing characteristic of the B-17G was the Bendix turret beneath the bombardier's position, but this feature, first tried on the X and YB-40 gunship, is also present on the final 86 B-17Fs produced. While the B-17G was to be the last production model of the Flying Fortress, the design by no means stagnated. Nose cheek gun installations continued to evolve, as did the waist gun positions – with the later B-17Gs featuring staggered, enclosed gun positions, at last giving the gunners the mobility and modicum of comfort they had needed from the outset.

The Sperry A-1 top turret was fitted with a higher Plexiglas dome with less framework, affording the gunner greater visibility and more headroom. The United Airlines Modification Center in Cheyenne, Wyoming, developed a new tail gun installation, since known as the Cheyenne Turret. The new installation provided notably better visibility for the gunner and increased flexibility of the twin .50 caliber machine guns, in addition to adding a reflector sight. It also reduced the length of the aircraft by five inches. The new tail gun installation began to be factory installed at B-17G-80-BO (43-28473), B-17G-55-VE (44-8287) and B-17G-25-DL (42-37989, but numerous other aircraft were retrofitted with the new mount at field modification centers in England.

The B-17G also had a pitot probe on the left side of the nose only. All of these changes resulted in a truly combat-worthy fighting machine, which when combined with the latest long-range fighter escort, was able to fulfill the Army Air Force's vision of strategic bombing.

A B-17G-60-DL of the 2nd Bomb Group, 15th Air Force, unloads a string of 500-pound bombs over a target in southern Europe. What appear to be boxes or packages are also streaming out of the bomb bay. The Fortress exhibits the staggered right waist window with a single laminated-glass pane, characteristic of later G-model B-17s. The last three digits of the serial number, 687, are painted below the front cheek window. (National Museum of the United States Air Force)

This Vega B-17G-1-VE bears serial number 42-39843 and a standard Olive Drab and Neutral Gray camouflage scheme. The national insignia has the Insignia White side bars and Insignia Red borders that were authorized for use from June to August 1943. At this point, the aircraft still has the deicer boots on the leading edges of the wings, stabilizer, and vertical tail. These deicer boots were deleted following lessons learned in combat. (Stan Piet collection)

Sergeant Mathis Finely of Metropolitan, Minnesota, uses a baking soda solution to scrub acid from the Plexiglas nose of a B-17G-10-VE, serial number 42-40011, of the 381st Bomb Group, 534th Bomb Squadron. The nickname *Schnozzle* and a caricature of comedian Jimmy Durante are painted on the fuselage. This aircraft suffered a midair collision with another B-17G named *Egg Haid* on 21 January 1945, with a loss of 18 crewmen. (National Archives)

Ground crewmen unload wooden crates of .50-caliber ammunition from a trailer during a replenishing operation on a B-17G, one of several Flying Fortresses nicknamed *Damfino*. Each crate held 350 rounds of M2 armor-piercing ammunition. At the far right is a crate of 1,500 rounds of .30-caliber ammunition, but it was evidently destined for another aircraft, since the B-17D was the last model to carry .30-caliber guns. (National Archives)

A flight of B-17s on a practice run over England includes in the foreground *Dreambaby*, B-17G-35-BO number 42-32025 of the 381st Bomb Group, 533rd Bomb Squadron. Its late-style tail turret was installed at Cheyenne, Wyoming, in January 1944. Cheek machine-gun window mounts were not installed on the early B-17Gs at the factories; the one on *Dreambaby* was a retrofit with a darker shade of Olive Drab on the frame. (National Archives)

Nine O Nine, a B-17G-30-BO, was named after the last three digits of her serial number, 42-31909. The USAAF accepted her on 15 December 1943, and she served with the 91st Bomb Group, 323rd Bomb Squadron, at Bassingbourn (Station 121), in Cambridgeshire, England. A ground crewman is painting another bomb on the fuselage, signifying one more completed mission. *Nine O Nine* completed 140 missions, reportedly the record for the Eighth Air Force.

Some of the small, painted bombs signifying *Nine O Nine*'s completed missions are visible in this photograph taken from the aircraft's left wing. The left chin machine gun window is a retrofit; its frame is a darker shade of Olive Drab than the color of the fuselage, and there is a slight overspray of that darker color onto the fuselage. The astrodome has been removed and replaced with a flat sheet of Plexiglas. After VE day, 909 returned to the States and was eventually scrapped at Kingman, Arizona.

Two aircrewmen inspect a chart in front of a B-17G. Visible inside the clear nose is the Olive Drab canvas cover over the Norden bombsight. Fitted to the slots for the machine gun barrels in the chin turret were zippered fabric covers to keep drafts from blowing into the turret. A ring around each barrel was linked to a zipper, so that as the guns were elevated or depressed, the zipper was pulled up or down, keeping the cover sealed shut. (National Archives)

This B-17G displays the dorsal turret introduced with the -G model, taller than the turrets of the preceding models. The configuration of the three cheek windows in the early B-17Gs is also demonstrated; the enlarged windows with gun mounts were reintroduced in later production blocks of the -G model. The chin turret is turned to the right, exposing the left and part of the right Plexiglas inspection/access panels on the rear of the turret. (Stan Piet collection)

Our Gal Sal was a B-17G-30-BO, serial number 42-31767. She served with the 100th Bomb Group, based at Thorpe Abbotts (Station 139), in Norfolk, England, and wore that group's tail insignia of a white square with a black D. At some point before this photograph was taken, the aircraft was retrofitted with cheek machine-gun window mounts. *Our Gal Sal* flew over 100 missions, with mission symbols being painted on both sides of the fuselage. (Stan Piet collection)

A closer view of *Our Gal Sal* highlights the aluminum color of the chin turret, which contrasts with the Olive Drab and Neutral Gray paint scheme on the rest of the aircraft. The frame of the front cheek window exhibits a different shade of paint than the fuselage, a characteristic of retrofitted windows. During a mission over Normandy on 8 August 1944, the plane suffered 38 FlaK holes but was repaired and sent back into combat. (Stan Piet collection)

This B-17G served with the 457th Bomb Group, 750th Bomb Squadron, based at Glatton (Station 130), Cambridgeshire, England, but was photographed at Mount Farm (Station 234), in Oxfordshire, in the summer of 1944. Organized 1 July 1943, this group flew its first mission on 21 February 1944, during "Big Week," and completed its final mission about two weeks before VE Day. The Plexiglas appears to be missing from the astrodome to the front of the cockpit. (Stan Piet collection)

The arrangement in which the waist guns were fired through large, open windows was changed in the B-17G to machine guns protruding through closed windows. The left waist mount is shown in this photo of a crewman cleaning his .50-caliber gun. The gun rested in a coil-spring equilibrator, visible in this photo at the opening in the window frame, which acted to stabilize the gun in a more or less neutral elevation. (National Archives)

A ground crewman removes the barrel from a .50-caliber machine gun in the chin turret of a B-17G of the 379th Bomb Group, 525th Bomb Squadron, on 2 March 1944. To perform this procedure, the barrel was pulled out of the rear of the gun, the slots in the bottom rear of the turret offering access openings for that purpose. The barrels were typically removed from the aircraft's turret guns for cleaning and maintenance after missions. (National Archives)

Personnel of the 381st Bomb Group at Ridgewell (Station 167), near Halstead in Essex, England, inspect an auxiliary fuel tank in front of a B-17G in January 1945. Up to two of these tanks, each with a capacity of about 400 U.S. gallons, could be mounted in the B-17G's bomb bay to give the aircraft extended range in ferrying missions; they could not be used in bombing missions. The original caption notes that the men were installing safety pins in the tank. (National Archives)

Mercy's Madhouse, B-17G-20-VE serial number 42-97557, of the 303rd Bomb Group, 358th Bomb Squadron, suffered a runway crash when the right main landing gear collapsed on its return from a training mission on 7 December 1944. *Mercy's Madhouse* was equipped at the factory with a PFF radome in place of the ball turret. This radar enabled the aircraft to carry out bombing missions in overcast weather. (National Museum of the United States Air Force)

Sugar, a Douglas B-17G-10-DL serial number 42-37721 of the 381st Bomb Group, 534th Bomb Squadron, is perched on a trailer headed for the salvage yard following a landing accident caused by the failure of the right main landing gear to lower. Although the right propellers were damaged, the left ones came through unscathed. The dorsal turret is an earlier type, rather than the type with the higher Plexiglas enclosure typically found on the B-17G. (National Archives)

Bombs have been delivered to a B-17G for the next mission. Fins have been installed on two of the bombs on the M5 bomb trailer, which is hitched to a Chevrolet 1 1/2-ton 4x4 M6 bomb-service truck. The trailer could hold up to 5,000 pounds of bombs and could be connected to other bomb trailers to form a train. The M6 bomb-service truck had a hand-operated hoist with a capacity of 4,000 pounds, for unloading the bomb trailer. (National Archives)

Actor Edward G. Robinson addresses a crowd of GIs in front of *Stage Door Canteen,* a Boeing-built B-17G-35-BO, serial number 42-31990. This Flying Fortress had been christened by Mary Churchill, the daughter of Winston Churchill, and named in honor of a famous servicemen's club in New York that also was the subject of a popular 1943 movie of the same name. On its fuselage was squadron/aircraft code MS-R. (Charles Bordner collection)

Stage Door Canteen is christened in London in April 1944. In addition to Mary Churchill, other celebrities present for the occasion included (left to right) Laurence Olivier, Alfred Lunt (carrying overcoat), and Olivier's wife, Vivien Leigh (visible toward the right). Newsreel footage shows Churchill breaking a champagne bottle over the left .50-caliber chin machine gun; it took her two hard strikes on the gun barrel to break the bottle. (Charles Bordner collection)

Mason and Dixon was a B-17G-15-BO (serial number 42-31412) with the 100th Bomb Group, 351st Bomb Squadron, based at Thorpe Abbots (Station 139), Norfolk, England. The Fortress was nicknamed after the Pilot, Buck Mason, and the navigator, Bill Dishion. The nose art was crafted by Sergeant Frank Stevens, a metal-shop worker in the group. The swastika below the nickname denotes a claim for a destroyed Luftwaffe aircraft.

Fletcher's Castoria, B-17G-5-BO serial number 43-31220, derived her nickname from dual sources: pilot Lieutenant William Fletcher and a brand of laxative. The aircraft's ball gunner, Pete Giaquinto, painted the nose art. This bomber was assigned to the 100th Bomb Group, 350th Bomb Squadron, and was the second B-17 in that squadron to carry the name *Fletcher's Castoria,* the first one having crashed during a training flight.

Lucky Stehley Boy, a B-17G of the 447th Bomb Group, sported matte blue cowls symbolic of the 711th Bomb Group. The nickname was painted in yellow over a four-leaf clover. Next to the nickname is a tribute to the "Victory" byword that was so important to the Allies in World War II: a yellow V, below which is painted the Morse code symbol for the letter V, dot-dot-dot-dash. Inside the V are two red bombs with white outlining.

Our Gal Sal featured the nose art of Sergeant Frank Stevens of the 100th Bomb Group. The aircraft was a B-17G-30-BO, serial number 42-31767, assigned to the 351st Bomb Squadron. She flew over 100 missions. The cheek gun mount was a retrofit, with a darker shade of Olive Drab having been applied to the frame. Factory-installed cheek mounts on Boeing B-17Gs would become standard with the -60 production block.

Stingy, B-17G-1-BO serial number 42-31053, began service with the 96th Bomb Group, 338th Bomb Squadron at Snetterton Heath (Station 138), Norfolk, England, in September 1943. "Singy" was the nickname of the son of Major General Fred Anderson, commander of the VIII Bomber Command. The bomber was lost in a mid-air collision over Woodend, England, 11 October 1944, with seven crewmembers perishing.

On 1 February 1945, Lieutenant John Kuhns, pilot of Male Call, B-17G-35-BO serial number 42-32102, of the 381st Bomb Group, 535th Bomb Squadron, had to abort a mission against Mannheim, Germany. He jettisoned his bombs over the Channel and made it back to his base at Ridgewell (Station 167), in Essex, England, where he crash-landed, slamming into a crew chief's hut. None of the crew was injured. (Charles Bordner collection)

Fools Rush In, B-17G-35-BO serial number 42-31987 of the 100th Bomb Group, 350th Bomb Squadron, had nose art by Sergeant Frank Stevens. On a combat mission on 31 December 1944, this aircraft collided and piggybacked with another B-17. All but two members of Fools Rush In survived the accident. The pilot on that mission, Captain Glenn Rojohn, who had also been the pilot of the B-17 that collided with Stingy in October 1944.

The nose art on Boots IV, a pair of winged cowboy boots with a red and white top hat inside a circle, was painted by Sergeant Johnnie White. A B-17G- serial number 42-37850 with the 96th Bomb Group, 337th Bomb Squadron, Boots IV was based at Snetterton Heath (Station 138), Norfolk, England, starting in October 1943. After flying at least 22 missions with the Eighth Air Force, Boots IV was transferred to the Fifteenth Air Force.

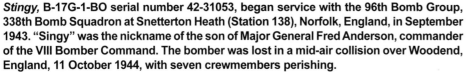

A Vega B-17G-40-VE, serial number 42-97991, with a protective covering over its waist-gun window flies over mountainous terrain. Visible is a cheek machine gun window mount, a feature omitted from the early B-17Gs but reintroduced with the B-17G-35-VE as well as the B-17G-60-BO and B-17G-25-DL. This Flying Fortress still retains the early-style tail turret rather than the Cheyenne tail turret. (Stan Piet collection)

The crew and VIP passengers of a 3rd Bombardment Division B-17G pose with some gifts the Soviets presented them during a stop on a shuttle mission to the USSR. This photograph illustrates that the early-type, non-staggered waist-gun positions were present on some bare-aluminum B-17Gs. Several styles of waist windows were in use on the B-17G, including this slightly bulged design with two oval and one rectangular clear panel. (National Archives)

Technical Sergeant Mexico J. Barraza, a gunner and radio operator, mans a .50-caliber machine gun in the waist of an Eighth Air Force B-17G. The waist window is an early-G-model type; its fixed design prevented air from entering the fuselage, adding immensely to the comfort of the gunners. Ammunition was fed to the guns through flexible chutes from large, wooden magazines. Below the gun is a canvas bag for collecting empty cartridges. (National Archives)

Boeing began delivering B-17Gs in bare-aluminum finish starting with the 114th aircraft in the -35 production block. This B-17G-45-BO, serial number 42-97229, reportedly gained its nickname, *Hi Ho Silver,* from the novelty of its unpainted, bright "silver" appearance. Assigned to the 379th Bomb Group, 524th Bomb Squadron, *Hi Ho Silver* was severely damaged in a midair collision in September 1944 and was discarded. (Stan Piet collection)

In the foreground, *Patches,* a B-17G-70-BO, serial number 43-37675, of the 381st Bomb Group, 532nd Bomb Squadron, has the Cheyenne tail turret that was installed at the United Air Lines Modification Center, Cheyenne, Wyoming, while the farther bomber, *Sleepy Time Gal,* B-17G-35-DL number 42-107112, has the earlier tail turret. Both aircraft have staggered waist windows of the late type featuring a single glass panel. (National Archives)

Queenie was B-17G-85-BO serial number 43-38382. She was delivered to the USAAF on 27 July 1944, and assigned to the 34th Bomb Group, 391st Bomb Squadron, Mendlesham, Suffolk, England, on 17 August 1944, flying her last mission 6 May 1945. In addition to the name *Queenie* painted over a red heart, an Olive Drab or green band was painted around the nose, and a shamrock was painted on the side of the chin turret.

Like *Queenie, Butch* was assigned to the 34th Bomb Group, 391st Bomb Squadron, at Mendlesham (Station 156). A B-17G-55-VE, this aircraft was assigned serial number 44-8271. The nose art consisted of a dragon blazing away with two machine guns while riding a bomb. *Butch* flew combat missions with the 34th Group from 17 September 1944 to 7 May 1945, following which the bomber was returned to the United States.

Seen at Rattlesden (Station 126), Suffolk, England, in mid-1945, *Blonde Bomber II,* a B-17G-90-BO serial number 43-38524, served in the Eighth Air Force with the 447th Bomb Group, 710th Bomb Squadron. To the front of the astrodome is the landing-approach antenna, part of a radio system that enabled the pilot to establish a bearing to an airfield. Over the pitot tube above the cheek turret is a cover with a pull-cord.

The nose art of B-17G-50-DL serial number 44-6483 of the 385th Bomb Group was the result of a contest by the U.S. military newspaper *Stars and Stripes* to find the most beautiful WAC (Women's Army Corps) in the European theater. Corporal Ruby Newell, a staff worker with the 3rd Bomb Division, was the winner, and Corporal James Ploss painted her likeness on the aircraft. *Ruby's Raiders* was lost in action in March 1945.

Dubbed *Humpty Dumpty,* this Flying Fortress with the 100th Bomb Group, serial number 42-107233, was the last B-17G-35-DL to leave the assembly line. The flex hose visible behind the clear nose is a deicer hose. Inside the top of the clear nose is the chin turret gun sight mount. The chin turret itself is a matte gray color. Visible through the cheek window are the .50-caliber machine gun receiver and the buffered gun cradle.

Ole-Timer served in the Eighth Air Force with the 34th Bomb Group, 18th Bomb Squadron. A B-17G-80-BO serial number 43-38138, this bomber flew its first combat mission on 17 September 1944. Although seriously damaged during a bombing mission on 5 November 1944, *Ole-Timer* was repaired and went on to fly more missions until its final sortie on 26 February 1945. The aircraft was returned to the States in June 1945.

A mechanic works on the number-two engine of *Boss Lady,* B-17G-55-BO serial number 42-102657 assigned to the 100th Bomb Group, 350th Bomb Squadron. On 11 September 1944, *Boss Lady* was badly shot up during an air battle over the Ore Mountains on the German-Czech border. Some of the crewmembers managed to bail out before the bomber exploded, the tail section crashing into the roof of a school in the Czech town of Kovářská.

Knockout Dropper was B-17G-80-VE serial number 44-8731, served first with the 332nd Bomb Squadron, 94th Bomb Group, then transferred to 34th Bomb Group, 4th Bomb Squadron on 26 January 1945. This bomber was outfitted as a pathfinder with H2X radar. It flew 22 operational missions and was on the records as an unused ground spare for an additional six missions before being returned to the United States in late December 1945. The nose art featured a nude woman in a cocktail glass.

Particularly stylish nose art by Sergeant Jay Cowan graced *Carolina Moon,* B-17G-75-BO serial number 43-37907 with the 490th Bomb Group. Bombs representing 66 of the 78 missions the bomber would eventually complete are painted on the fuselage. There is also a swastika, representing one German aircraft killed. Details are visible of the crew access hatch, the cheek gun mount, and the clear inspection panels at the rear of the chin turret. (Stan Piet collection)

Another racy example of Sergeant Jay Cowan's nose art was found on *Looky Looky,* a Flying Fortress of the 490th Bomb Group, 851st Bomb Squadron. The bomber was a B-17G-70-DL, serial number 44-6893. In addition to the landing approach antenna to the front of the astrodome on the deck in front of the windshield, there is a whip antenna and an antenna mast aft of the astrodome. A protective wrapping is on the cheek-gun barrel. (Stan Piet collection)

A Chevrolet M6 bomb-service truck has hauled a load of 500-pound bombs to a B-17G of the 91st Bomb Group. Two M5 bomb trailers are hitched in tandem, with the rear trailer positioned under the front of the fuselage. All of the fins have been fitted on the bombs on both trailers. To the right, a mechanic in a shearling jacket makes adjustments to the number-one engine, the cowl section of which lies on the tarmac. (Stan Piet collection)

Ground crewmen ready a B-17G for a mission. To the left, a mechanic lies atop the number-three engine, making a final check. To the front of the cockpit, a crewman has removed the astrodome and is standing up through the opening. Another man is polishing the Plexiglas nose. On the ground, armorers fasten the fins on 2,000-pound bombs prior to bombing-up the Flying Fortress. (National Archives)

Little Miss Mischief, B-17G-35-VE serial number 42-97880, with the 91st Bomb Group, 324th Bomb Squadron, crashed during takeoff for a mission on in 4 April 1945. The chin turret and the fuselage around it were crumpled, and the propellers were bent. Salvage operations were already underway; inflatable rubber bladders had lifted the aircraft, and caterpillar tracks had been inserted under the wings for towing the bomber away. (National Archives)

This 100th Bomb Group Flying Fortress sustained damage on 7 April 1945, when a Messerschmitt Bf 109 with a dead pilot in the cockpit crashed into the tail. Slashes made by the Messerschmitt's propeller are visible on the vertical stabilizer and fuselage. Despite the catastrophic damage, this Fort, like so many others, made it back to England. She was a B-17G-90, serial number 43-38514, with a Cheyenne tail turret.

A Bit O' Lace, B-17G-40-VE serial number 42-97976, with the 447th Bomb Group, 709th Bomb Squadron, was damaged by FlaK over Kiel, Germany, on 4 April 1945, peppering the rudder and vertical stabilizer with rips and holes and severing most of the left horizontal elevator and stabilizer. The group's symbol, a K in a square, was surrounded by yellow on the vertical stabilizer, with bare aluminum behind the serial number.

Crew Chief Master Sergeant William A. Lucas of Ashland, Wisconsin, cleans out the spent-cartridge ejector chute of a Cheyenne turret on a B-17G. The turret incorporated a laterally swiveling ball, with the .50-caliber machine guns elevating and depressing through the slots in the ball. This example lacks the large, curved external armor unit installed on some Cheyenne turrets that formed a protective tub for the tail gunner. (National Archives)

Three crewmen from *The Peacemaker,* B-17G-65-BO serial number 43-37552, of the 91st Bomb Group, 401st Bomb Squadron, inspect battle damage to their aircraft after returning to their base at Bassingbourn (Station 121), in Cambridgeshire, England. The two aviators to the right are wearing AN-S-31 summer flying suits, over which the lieutenant to the right is wearing a Type A2 summer flying jacket. He also has on Type A6 shearling flying boots. (National Archives)

Preparing for the eventuality of a ditching, three B-17 gunners conduct dinghy drill in England: (left to right) Staff Sergeant Henry J. Hall, Technical Sergeant Gail R. Darner, and Staff Sergeant Anthony P. Pizzonia. Darner is operating the SCR-578, an emergency transmitter powered by a hand crank on top. On front of the unit is a reel for the wire antenna. This radio sent out a signal (SOS or keyed messages) enabling rescue crews to locate the craft. (National Archives)

The B-17's Wright Cyclone engines were dependable power plants, but they had a finite service life, and they were subject to damage in battle or from exceeding the engines' limitations. Helping remove an engine unit from a B-17 prior to installation of a new engine is Sergeant Leslie Unruh. The unit included the engine, mount (part of which is visible to the lower rear of the unit), and accessories, for ease of removal and installation. (National Archives)

A ground crewman surveys damage to a B-17. Judging from the badly bent propellers, the aircraft probably made an emergency, wheels-up landing with the engines running. Remnants of a Hamilton Standard logo decal are on the lower blade, outboard of the white stencil with the blade's part number (6477A-0) and serial number. The corporal is wearing a first-pattern ETO lined field jacket, locally manufactured in England (National Archives)

The 5,000th Flying Fortress produced by Boeing after the Japanese attack on Pearl Harbor came in for special honors. Dubbed *5 Grand,* B-17G-70-BO serial number 43-37716 became in effect a giant autograph book for those who worked on her construction. On 13 March 1944, a Boeing worker, Mrs. Gertrude Aldrich, whose son had perished in a B-17, christened the aircraft by breaking a champagne bottle on the chin turret. (National Archives)

During an exhibit at the Boeing factory featuring *5 Grand,* the aircraft is bedecked with signs drawing attention to her significance. The names of workers who participated in her construction were painted on virtually every spare inch of the aircraft, an exception being the control surfaces. During early flights of *5 Grand,* it was discovered that the hundreds of painted signatures created drag, slowing down the aircraft by several miles per hour. (Air Force Historical Research Agency)

Women workers put the final touches on *5 Grand* on a hardstand at the Boeing factory. The plane's nickname was painted in black with a buff yellow border. Names of personnel were painted in a multitude of sizes and colors, leading some to give the plane the additional nickname "the Easter egg." As a Boeing promotional project, *5 Grand* was meant to commemorate and honor those who built her and the B-17s that preceded her. (Air Force Historical Research Agency)

So many Boeing workers clamored to get their names on *5 Grand* that some of them painted them over existing names. Signatures came in all sizes. Some signed their full names, while others lettered in just a first name or nickname. For emphasis, some drew an outline around their name. Protective covers have been wrapped around the .50-caliber gun barrel cooling sleeves, to protect the bare metal from corrosion until delivered. (Air Force Historical Research Agency)

5 Grand displays her unit symbol, a C in a black square, while with the 96th Bomb Group, 338th Bomb Squadron, in England. By this time, a few signatures had been added to the rudder. Despite suffering a crash landing in August 1944, she completed 78 combat missions. Following a war bond tour in the States after VE Day, *5 Grand* was sent to Kingman, Arizona, where she was scrapped along with thousands of other surplus planes.

This B-17G was one of a number of radar-equipped pathfinder aircraft assigned to 401st Bomb Group at Deenethorpe (Station 128), Northamptonshire, England. In place of the ball turret is an H2X radome, seen here in the retracted position. These devices were called "Mickey Mouse," later shortened to "Mickey." Pathfinders could pinpoint a ground target through thick clouds, alerting bombers following behind them when to drop their bomb loads. (Stan Piet collection)

The last Flying Fortress produced by Boeing, the 6,981st, received a similar commemorative treatment to that accorded 5 Grand. This B-17G was covered with bomb-shaped labels listing the hundreds of enemy towns and cities B-17s had attacked in all theaters. Another photo of this aircraft shows that she had labels dated as late as March 1945. In the background is a B-29 displaying labels for Japanese cities struck. (Air Force Historical Research Agency)

This B-17G-35-DL, serial number 42-107092, landed at Dübendorf, Switzerland, on 31 July 1944. The aircraft, piloted by Second Lieutenant Jay Ossiander, was assigned to the 401st Bomb Group, 615th Bomb Squadron, and was based out of Deenethorp, Northamptonshire. It was one of the first four natural aluminum-finished aircraft to be based at that field. The nose art and aircraft name differed from side to side, with *Umbriago* on the right and *Freckles* on the left.

Introduced in 1945, the B-17H was the B-17G modified for air-sea rescue operations. Testing of the concept began in November 1943, and on 10 June 1944 Higgins Industries of New Orleans was awarded a sole-source contract to produce 600 of the A-1 airborne lifeboat. This order was subsequently reduced to 300, and 130 of the B-17H were order converted from B-17Gs. The first actual rescue by a B-17H took place off the coast of Denmark in April of 1945. While during WWII the B-17H carried no distinguishing markings, after the war the aircraft began to wear the standardized rescue markings of the Army, Navy, and new Air Force. In 1948 it was redesignated the SB-17G. It carried a jettisonable, twin-engined, 27-foot Higgins A-1 lifeboat under the fuselage and frequently a search radar in the location formerly occupied by the chin turret. This SB-17G, serial number 44-83773, seen flying over Diamond Head, Oahu. Hawaii, is wearing the broad yellow bands with black borders used after WWII to signify rescue aircraft. (Larry Davis collection)

An SB-17G from the 10th Rescue Squadron cruises over mountainous terrain in Alaska. The serial number, 43-39437, indicates that this aircraft was converted from a B-17G-110-BO. The procedure for delivering the lifeboat was to drop it from about 1,500 feet directly over the personnel to be rescued. A static line deployed a parachute on the boat. When the boat touched down, rockets on it were fired, deploying lifelines to the sides. (National Museum of the United States Air Force)

This B-17H bears the new national insignia with red bars introduced in 1947 and the markings of Flight D, 5th Rescue Squadron, Air Rescue Service. The Higgins lifeboat was made of laminated mahogany and weighed 3,300 pounds. Able to cruise up to 1,500 miles, the boat carried a radio and provisions enough for 12 people to survive for 20 days. The lifeboat's 20 watertight compartments made the boat nearly impossible to sink or capsize. (National Museum of the United States Air Force)

An SB-17G, serial number 44-85746, makes a stop in the al-Rub' al-Khâlî desert, Saudi Arabia, in 1950. Slots have been cut in the bomb bay doors, presumably to accommodate the lifeboat-mounting equipment. This SB-17G crashed on the Olympic Peninsula in Washington State on 19 January 1952, on its way back to McChord Field from a search-and-rescue mission. The crash resulted in the loss of three crewmen. (National Museum of the United States Air Force)

But for use as target drones, the final military use of the B-17 by the United States Air Force took place in Southeast Asia. TB-17G-95-VE serial number 44-85531 was photographed at Clark Air Base in the Philippines in October 1957, while conducting clandestine operations. Remarkably, one of the alleged reasons the B-17 was chosen for this service is that its silhouette reportedly did not "look" like an American plane to peoples of the area. (Larry Davis collection)

Landing gear extended and the sun about to set, a B-17 Flying Fortress of the Eighth Air Force comes in for a landing at her home base in England following a combat mission over northwestern Europe. Time after time, B-17s demonstrated the ability to fly tremendous distances, brave clouds of FlaK and fighters, absorb terrible damage, and yet deliver their bomb loads with precision and return safely to base. The longer ranges required in the Pacific, plus the development of the atom bomb, meant that with the capitulation of the Third Reich, the sun had set on the Flying Fortress's days as a bomber. (National Archives)